THE ART OF CREATIVE SONGWRITING

THE ART OF CREATIVE SONGWRITING
A Songwriter's Handbook

Stephanie Bruce

Copyright © 2022 by Stephanie Bruce

All rights reserved. No part of this publication may be reproduced, stored in a retrieval system, or transmitted, in any form or by any means, except as may be expressly permitted by the 1976 Copyright Act or by the copyright holder in writing.

ISBN: 978-1-78324-258-0

Whilst every effort has been made to ensure that the information contained within this book is correct at the time of going to press, the author and publisher can take no responsibility for the errors or omissions contained within.

Published and book design by
wordzworth.com

*Dedicated to the many music teachers
who imparted their knowledge and wisdom,
giving me the keys to this world of wonders.*

CONTENTS

Preface		xi
Introduction		xiii
1	**The Feels**	**1**
	Exercise 1: Name that Feeling	*4*
2	**Getting Started**	**9**
	Exercise 2: A Practical Process	*11*
	Expand Your Choices	*13*
	For Example	*17*
3	**Lyrics**	**19**
	Honesty	*19*
	Content and Method	*20*
	Rhythm in Words	*21*
	Sensory Imagery	*22*
	Nouns and Adjectives	*23*
	Verbs and Adverbs	*24*
	Actual Feelings	*24*
	To Rhyme or Not to Rhyme?	*25*
	Similes and Metaphors	*26*
	Exercise 3: Complete the Following Sentences	*27*
	Alliteration and Repetition	*27*
	Impressionism	*28*
	Simplicity	*29*
	Humor	*30*

	The Sound of Words	*30*
	Dynamic Sequence	*31*
	Visit the Masters	*32*
	Exercise 4: Analysis of Lyrics You Love	*34*
4	**Melody**	**41**
	Default Melody	*41*
	Melody Rich Music	*42*
	TA: Scale Degrees and Chords	*43*
	Melodic Variations	*45*
	Melodic Motif	*47*
	The Blues Scale	*47*
	Singability	*48*
	Melodies without Chords	*48*
	The Low and High of It	*49*
	Beyond Scale Tones: Many More Colors	*49*
	Exercise 5: Adding Melody to a Chord Progression	*50*
5	**Harmony**	**55**
	Chord Progressions	*56*
	TA: Scale Tone Chords	*56*
	Chord Extensions	*57*
	Functional Harmony	*59*
	Secondary Dominants and Blues Chords	*61*
	Reharmonizing	*62*
	Pedal Point and Slash Chords	*63*
	Non-Functional Slash Chords	*65*
	Chromatic/Non-Functional Harmony	*65*
	Modulation	*68*
	But Do You Love It?	*70*
	Exercise 6: Adding Chords to a Melody	*70*

6	**Rhythm**	**75**
	Groove Driven Music	*75*
	Time Signature	*76*
	Quarter Note Subdivisions	*77*
	Straight 8th Grooves	*78*
	Triplet Based Grooves	*78*
	16th Note Subdivision	*80*
	Hybrid Grooves and Layering	*81*
	Tempo	*82*
	Syncopation	*83*
	Rubato	*84*
	Percussion	*85*
	Singing the Groove	*85*
	Exercise 7: Playing with Rhythm	*86*
7	**Form**	**91**
	How Does Form Work?	*91*
	Components of Form in Songs	*92*
	Form in Action	*95*
	Beyond Tradition	*96*
	Song Length	*97*
	Exercise 8: Analysing Form	*98*
8	**Presentation**	**105**
	Do You Love It?	*105*
	Musical Notation	*106*
	Charts	*107*
	Reading the Map (See Example above)	*109*
	Notation Software	*110*
	Demo Recording	*110*
	The Impact of Good Singing	*111*
	Arranging	*112*

	Studio Recording	113
	Video: The Industry Standard for Sharing Your Work	114
	Performing Your Songs	116
	Sales: The Big Hustle	117
	Exercise 9: Perform Your Song	118
9	**Coda**	**123**
	Songwriting Methods and Instruction	123
	The Hack	125
	The Hook: Is It Necessary?	125
	Collaboration	127
	Rewriting and Discarding	127
	Grow Your Skills	128
	Criticism	129
	Copyright	130
	The Younger Generation	130
	Talent	132
	Finally	134
Appendix		135
	Songwriters (Composer/Lyricists)	136
	Songwriting Teams	140
	Lyricists	142
Resources		145
Thank You		147
About the Author		149

PREFACE

I have been writing songs for over 50 years. No one taught me how to do it, but I fell in love with the music that singer/songwriters were creating when I was a teenager in the 1960s. I played the piano and the guitar, loved to sing, and was thrilled when I heard the music of Joni Mitchell and Laura Nyro. The songs I wrote were a million miles from the level of talent, imagination, and craft evident in the songs my idols were writing, but I kept doing it. Years passed before I began performing and recording my original tunes. I studied music and practiced, expanding my skills and vocabulary, and over the years found my own voice as a songwriter. Spending a couple of decades singing jazz, I learned about the language of music, and was captivated by the mysterious beauty of jazz harmony and melody. Singing the standards of Tin Pan Alley gave me a strong sense of structure, and harmonic vocabulary. When I became a music teacher it was important to me to impart to my vocal students that being a good singer also meant being a good musician.

When I began teaching songwriting, I searched for a method book that covered the material that was important to me as a songwriter. I couldn't find one. Though some contained considerable valuable information, most of the books I saw were oriented toward pop music and a formulaic approach to writing "hit" songs. I wrote this book with the intention of providing a handbook for songwriters who are interested in music that is not necessarily commercially popular but leans toward personal originality, musical curiosity, strong musicianship, authenticity, intentional craft, and a willingness to explore. The book is a tool for intermediate/advanced songwriters who know their way around an instrument and the fundamentals of music theory.

This is not a textbook and what I offer is not songwriting pedagogy. This is my personal perspective, and everything I have to say here is based on my own education and experience as a working musician, instructor, and writer of songs. As a singer I have loved performing hundreds of well-written songs over the years, marveling at the work of the great songwriters. I hope my experiences nudge the reader to explore sounds that are unfamiliar, to try new things, rhythms and melodies, chord progressions, and flexible forms. I'm not a music scholar and admit to being very opinionated about what I like and don't like. Everything I suggest is an approach I have used in my own songwriting, and most of what I know about music came to me through listening to music I love. When I had questions, I found teachers. We have all listened to plenty of music, and songwriters start by copying the songs we love, which is the real education.

Every chapter in the book contains sub-headings labeling specific information. I assume the reader has enough familiarity with musical notation to understand what I mean (though I have included some refresher info about theory). The many examples of musical ideas should be played at the piano for maximum benefit. I'm not dogmatic in telling my readers what music they should love or emulate, but this book offers some alternate approaches to the current body of available songwriting instruction. I also include exercises the reader can try, and a short list of abbreviated tips that might help at various points along the way in this multi-dimensional endeavor.

Words written about music are not music. When you come to a section in the book that includes musical notation, please play it. It will mean nothing unless you hear it. When songs are mentioned, please listen to them. Every song listed in the book is available online, either through your music streaming platform, or Youtube. You want to write good songs? Listen to good songs. Every song mentioned here is worthy of your time and listening to them will expand your comprehension of what makes a song good. It may seem like songwriting is a lot of work, but remember, when playing music, the emphasis is on *playin*g. Writing songs is fun, so enjoy your explorations, your experiments, the words and sounds that come through, and the present time process of adding the spark of life to your musical stories.

INTRODUCTION

What is a song? The Harper's Dictionary of Music says: "…a short musical composition for solo voice, with or without instrumental accompaniment…" That's a brief and concise definition, but let's expand it a little. A song is a relatively short musical composition written for the voice, which is comprised of these elements: melody, harmony, rhythm, form, and lyrics. In the pages that follow, we will be looking at all aspects of songwriting, individually, and how they work together to create the alchemy of a satisfying piece of vocal music. In addition to the musical composition, and the creation and crafting of meaningful lyrics, we'll also look at some of the available options for releasing your songs into the listening world.

Many songwriting books and courses offer you a formula for writing "hit songs". Authors and teachers have compiled the lists of frequently used chord progressions, approaches to rhyme, common tempos and forms, melodic dynamics, etc., as found in popular songs, old and new. The assumption is that following the tried and true will result in songs that sound like the ones you hear on the radio, in movies, in live performances, sung by popular artists who are famous and make a lot of money. Sometimes the definition of a good song seems to be that it sounds like somebody more famous than you wrote it. This is precisely what some songwriters are aiming for, especially if they are beginners. Many experienced songwriters are making careers out of writing popular music for famous singers and bands, or songs that are placed in movies and television shows. Some of the songs that make it at this level are truly exceptional. I have nothing but respect for anyone's ability to have a lucrative career as a professional songwriter and I'm a big fan of great pop tunes. Some of my favorite songs have achieved "hit" status because they are well written and performed and have been played for decades since they first hit the air waves. But more often momentary "wannabe" hits live briefly in our sonic awareness, if at all, before being cast into the bin of forgettable songs. The writers may have followed all the rules of good songwriting, but somehow missed the most important thing. The music doesn't make you feel anything. Genuine, deep feeling has always been the centerpiece of my inspiration, the reason for taking the time and energy to commit to writing a song.

When you are just starting your songwriting adventure, the way to learn how it all works is to imitate. If you are reading this, you have already heard a zillion songs, played and sung many of them, know which ones you like, which ones you think are stupid, and which ones make your heart explode with rapture. There are probably songs that make you think (as I often do), "I wish I had written that." Imitation is often the pathway to originality. Becoming familiar with common practice approaches to songwriting expands your awareness of how songs are put together. Things like, what to write about, what kind of chords to use, how sections of songs work together to create movement and balance, dynamic high points, how to tell a story in lyrics, what a "hook" is, what makes you want to sing along. There are many other things that you probably don't really think about when you listen to a song, but you may have integrated these elements without realizing it before you write your first song.

I would like to help you to experience what might be possible in the creation of songs that are not limited to the function of commercial music. I would not presume to give you a definition of "artistic" music, but in my own work, I aim to write songs that are not only fun to listen to and perform, but are also emotionally dimensional, musically imaginative, carefully crafted, representative of individual authenticity, and not bound by the rules of writing hits. There are audiences out there who are excited by music that is adventurous and fresh, songs that move beyond established conventions. For some listeners, the most captivating, soul satisfying music is very different from the songs that are popular in the mainstream and is often created by artists you've never heard of.

I wrote my first song when I was 17 years old. I can't remember one thing about it except that I performed it only once, at my first gig in a little church coffeehouse in West Seattle. I was playing guitar and singing a lot of folk songs in those days, and I'm sure my song was as close as I could get to copying the music I was listening to. But making up an actual song, with words, chords, melody, and form, was a monumental accomplishment for me back then. It was my first step on the path to becoming a lifetime songwriter, and I am still writing songs many decades later. Over the years, my process has evolved considerably. While I spent the first couple of decades doing my best to copy my idols, I eventually discovered that I had my own voice. This is a big turning point for anyone working in any facet of the arts. When you stop thinking "What would Joni Mitchell do here?", and start trusting your own thoughts, feelings, and musical preferences, songwriting becomes a very precious gift – to yourself and hopefully, to your audiences.

As we embark on this songwriting expedition, my best advice is this: Love what you do. When you write a song, do it with love and devotion. Learn to trust your own ears, your own preferences, and don't be afraid to be bold, to try new things. Once you have an idea and begin to write, don't stop working on your song until you are in love with it. Love the finished outcome because you are certain it is the very best you can do, the very best musical expression of your inspiration you can possibly create. If your song is almost there, but one chord isn't right, or a lyrical phrase is awkward, mundane, or only half true, change it. Work on it until you love every note, every word, every chord, and every aspect of form. Love your work so that every time you sing your song, it fills you with elation and sparkly, electric, satisfaction. Love it so much you know it's good. And if you get the chance to perform it, it's okay if some of your listeners' responses are lukewarm. If you love your song, and love the songwriting process, you have tapped into a rare and precious energy. You have expanded your soul and your place in the cosmos in a way that only art can do. This is The Art of Creative Songwriting.

1
THE FEELS

The feeling a song evokes is the most important thing about it. Music is powerful stuff, and it can produce a full spectrum of emotions. We turn to music because it enhances and intensifies our feelings, whether we feel like crying, driving down the coast with the top down, or falling in or out of love. One of the primary reasons why human beings engage in any aspect of the arts, either as a creator or a member of the audience, is to experience emotion. We want to feel something. Music is often functional, lost in the rest of the noise, influencing us to buy more if we are shopping, eat faster in a restaurant, feel more relaxed waiting to see the dentist, burn through the pain while running, or make us funnier and sexier while drinking in a bar. In situations like these, we may not even be aware of what the music is. The sonic texture of background music often seems to blend with the décor of the room. We all know the experience of having to listen to music we don't like, which can feel like torture. But some of the music we love is meant to be heard without any other distractions, on a concert stage, or alone with a killer sound system, to be wept over in the shadowy corners of the heart, celebrated in the cathedrals of the spirit, or shared up close in the eyes of a loved one, savored, understood, and embraced, again and again. Music this good is best experienced as the main attraction and doesn't require additional entertainment to keep us interested.

A great song can be a very sophisticated composition, or a simple melody with an unadorned lyric. It can be wildly adventurous, unconventional, poetic and refined, or something a child can sing by ear. The writer may have worked long and hard, impeccably following all the rules of songwriting, or may have allowed the song to spill out in an hour, with no attention whatsoever to issues of correct songcraft. A truly memorable song, one that gets under your skin, captures in words and music the essence of authentic feeling. Music is energy, and the energy of sound can be shaped into powerful stories about the time we spend here on planet Earth. And let's face it – life is emotional. As Maya Angelou said, what we remember most about people is the way they make us feel. We remember songs for the same reason.

One of the problems we attempt to solve in the pursuit of a good song is finding the balance between true inspiration and craft. You can fool a lot of people a lot of the time, and that's often the case in popular music. We've all heard songs that sound like they were factory made. The writer may have understood the mechanics of music but they were not necessarily inspired by personal emotion in the song. Songcraft without substance is a big part of the musical landscape in many genres and this is nothing new. Songs created in this way are like those old paint-by-number pictures we had in the 1950s when I was a kid (young readers are going, "huh?"). Every shape in the picture was numbered and each number had a corresponding color. When you followed the directions correctly, you could paint a landscape of mountains and trees rising above a lake, or a lady with a big hat. It was especially good if you squinted your eyes to blur the borders between the shapes, which would then look like real shadows and light. Follow the directions and create a painting. Follow the rules of songwriting and create a song. If your intention is to make something that looks like a painting, or sounds like a song, following the rules might get you there, and many listeners will be none the wiser. But this approach is worlds away from feeling something authentic and then writing about it in a thoroughly contemplated and honest way. A beautiful photograph of food does not satisfy your hunger. A picture of a horse galloping over the hills will not make your hair blow back in the wind. Craft is still important, especially when it is used to mine and refine ideas that rise out of your center. Countless songs express deep emotional honesty while adhering to the conventions of style, but we also have many choices beyond stylistic forms. If you aspire to create music that is a unique expression of your life, your experiences, your travels around the sun, the people you have met and loved along the way, and the prism of your responses to them, consider moving beyond the common practice templates. Take the time to explore what you feel and want to say. It doesn't matter how many songs you write. When we go for quality over quantity, one good song is worth more than zillions of mediocre ones.

So, where do we find true feelings to write about? It may seem that writing from an emotional place means heavy drama, (I love you so much I can't stand it, I used to love you until you did that thing, you used to love me, my heart is broken, we are the world, brother can you spare a dime, etc.) But emotion comes to us many times a day, in little moments, places, memories, sensory impressions, and surprising encounters. Have you ever been out walking and noticed how the play of light on the leaves of a big tree reminded you of when you were young, running through the neighborhood, feeling free and full of life? How do you feel now when you look at the contrast of your life as an adult? Do you miss your carefree youth, or are you glad to have gained the wisdom of age? How did it feel when your heart was broken the first time? How has your impression of romance changed over the years? Or have you found that romantic love has given way to a more loving acceptance of who you are right now? If you are paying attention to your life, you will find things to write about. The range of topics is as broad as everything you care about, from the profound grief of lost love to fun, lighthearted things, like riding a bicycle on a summer day. And because we are working in the medium of music and lyrics, you don't have to name the feeling you are describing. Your song may evoke a mood that is multidimensional, balancing what is said with what is implied, transporting your listeners into a dreamscape, or something long forgotten, a mysterious soul stirring longing. Anything meaningful to you can be the subject of an original song, and the best songs are loaded with the juice of living.

We might seem to be dealing with only the verbal aspects of songwriting, but a song is comprised of lyrics and music. I have seen instructors coaching students in lyric writing, and while they may help a writer refine and shape the lyrics into verse and chorus, meter and rhyme, they often neglect the musical part of the story. What you hear then is a clever and well-crafted lyric set to a mundane melody and chord changes. Songwriters with a broad musical vocabulary equal to their verbal fluency have many more choices for approaching their songs with creativity. Poetry can be profoundly moving, and music can lift us to the outer galaxies. Put them together with intention, inspiration, and impeccable attention to the details of craft, and you may end up with a song that is better than a "hit". One of the greatest compliments I have received is when someone comes up to me after a concert and tells me one of my songs made them cry. They have no idea how many hours of composing, rewriting, editing, revising, and revisiting went into creating the finished song, but the centerpiece of the experience for them is what it made them feel. They don't necessarily realize that I take every minute detail of songwriting seriously and never settle for place holders. If I don't love all of it, it isn't finished yet. If I don't cry, or whoop with joy when it's complete, I didn't get there, and the song will probably go into the "unfinished" file.

In the coming chapters we're going to look at all aspects of songwriting. We will visit the fundamentals of common practice in popular music, but you will be invited to explore meticulously the subjects you write about, to hunt for the treasure of distilled, emotion-rich ideas, and to depict them in ways that are bold in bending the rules and conventions of popular songs. If this sounds like musical anarchy, rest assured we are still aiming for well-crafted cohesiveness in our songs. The options are endless, from intro to ending, and like so many things in life, the freedom you enjoy in fully expressing yourself is probably best contained within a disciplined framework of sound musical and lyrical principles. You will be encouraged to try without fear of failure, knowing that rewriting or discarding and starting over are part of the process. Throw it at the wall and see what sticks. If half of it falls to the floor, we can always clean up the mess. Just remember to keep going back and checking in with what is meaningful and beautiful to you, rather than aiming only to fit the popular template.

Exercise 1: Name that Feeling

Read each subject listed here. Stop for a few minutes and see if there are feelings that come up in relation to the topics. If the item listed doesn't evoke emotion, move on to the next. Write a sentence or two describing the essence of the feelings that emerge.

1. You're a teenager, running through a cemetery on a warm, dark summer night, with someone you are crazy attracted to, but haven't kissed yet. Will you make your move?
2. You tried to do something that really mattered to you, but you couldn't achieve what you were going for. You need to talk to someone who loves you unconditionally, someone who will help put you back together.
3. There is a place you like to go alone. It may be a noisy city street, a quiet place in the woods, a beach that's right on the ocean, a bell tower with a dazzling view, a room of your own that is always there. What does being there feel like?
4. You're trying to decide whether to stay or go. The relationship might have a future if you hang in, or it might be better to cut your losses and hope that someone else who is better for you will come along.

There were some older girls in my neighborhood, already in high school, when I was 8 or 9 years old. They let me hang around with them sometimes when they got together to listen to 45rpm records from the top ten hits of the day. There was a song that was a big smash, by a group of guys called The Four Seasons. The lead singer had a high voice with a powerful edge. I remember the song, "Sherry", which was a typical teen love song, and the way the singer would wail, "She-e-e-e-er-ry Bay-yay-be.." It just killed me. I knew nothing about romance and sex, but the sound of his voice, the energy and urgency of his longing, crying out to the girl of his dreams, to please "come out tonight", transported me to another world. We played the song over and over, line dancing in the little basement rec room. The older girls whispered and giggled about boys they had crushes on, while I just wanted to hear the song again. It made me feel something I couldn't really describe, something very vibrant and exciting. It was certainly far more captivating than the simple pieces I played on the piano for my weekly lessons in the basement of the convent at Holy Rosary School.

I gradually lost interest in piano lessons altogether. My fingers could find the notes on the keyboard, and I could keep time, but it wasn't very fun. Somehow the nuns just didn't get it. I was about 10 years old when the kids in the neighborhood went together to the Admiral Theater to see "West Side Story". After seeing that film, I knew life would never again be the same, and music became the ultimate wonderland of fantasy and feeling. My school uniform, navy blue pleated skirt and a white middy blouse with a navy tie, became an object of scorn. After seeing boys in tight jeans leaping around on a playground to the music of Leonard Bernstein, their cool attitudes and graceful toughness became our new religion. We, like kids all over America, memorized the songs and sang them endlessly, jumping around wildly in fake dance moves while snapping our fingers. I had no idea who Sondheim and Bernstein were, but this music was an elixir. The intensity of the thrill was almost unbearable and ignited in me a craving for life with a soundtrack, one that gripped my heart, made me laugh, made me weep, and informed me that childhood was ending. I did not know at the time music would become my path, or that "West Side Story" would be considered a masterpiece, but I was crazy hooked on it. It didn't matter what the notes were. It only mattered that this language touched the core of my young, preteen soul. It was all about the feeling. And you know what? I still revere the show, and most of my musician friends agree.

Tips

1. Sharpen and expand your awareness of what you love about the music you listen to most. Fine tune your observation of details that make a song great for you. Don't stop at "I love that song". Ask yourself why you love it.

2. If you are attracted to a song because of the way it makes you feel, notice the elements of the composition that evoke a strong emotional response. Is it the lyrics? The melody? The groove? The chords? A combination of ingredients that is greater than the sum of its parts? If you aren't doing this already, pay attention to the little things that elevate a song to its place in the soundtrack of your life.

3. There are songs you like, songs you don't notice, songs that aggravate you, and songs that send you over the moon, in rapture, in tears, in the urge to dance, or gaze into the eyes of your beloved. Make a list of songs, 20 or so, that you would place as contenders in the "Best Songs of All Time" contest. With each title, ask yourself why this song is so special.

2
GETTING STARTED

When you decide to write a song, to start from scratch with no specific idea or feeling to express, you might go to your instrument, maybe piano or guitar, and sit there for a while waiting for inspiration to strike. You fool around with a few chords, play a song you already know, wait awhile, noodle some more on your strings or keys, and if nothing wells up from within, you may be inclined to think it's just not a good day for songwriting. You put down the guitar, or get up from the piano, and decide to go out and take a walk.

You stroll down the city streets and let your mind wander as the world enters through your senses. Your present time perceptions will include the smells of car exhaust, food cooking, a cigarette, the perfume of someone walking by. You will notice the buildings you pass, the shapes of the clouds, and how the leaves on the trees that line the sidewalk make patterns of shade on the concrete. Somebody walks by who reminds you of your grandmother, and then you notice a young couple arguing as a kid zooms by on a skateboard. You stop at a coffee bar and buy a cup, noticing the dark aroma and flavor of the brew. An old vintage car drives by with windows rolled down, and you can hear Bob Dylan's "Like a Rolling Stone" pouring out from the radio at top volume. The air is just the right temperature, warm with a slight breeze blowing across your skin, and perhaps a little a city grit hits the back of your throat. As you let your mind enjoy these impressions, you look up at an open window with a faded lace curtain blowing out over the frame. A woman stands watching, partially hidden by the lace. Her face is expressionless, but when she sees you looking at her, she smiles. She reminds you of someone. That someone was a character in a play about your life. The play is called "My Actual Life". Effortlessly, a phrase appears, a few words that encapsulate the feeling that rises when you think about a scene in your memory, and the person who once meant something to you. Luckily, you have some paper and a pen, and you walk over to the nearest parked car to use as a desktop, and you start writing. She has opened the door to your memory and something about her will be the subject of your next song.

The woman in the window reminds you of someone you once knew, but that doesn't tell us much about why the person from your past mattered to you. Can you tell us what it was that made that person so memorable that a stranger looking out the window took you back to another time in your life that was charged with feeling? What was your relationship with the woman? Which time period of your life? Where were you? Can you recall sensory impressions that describe the time and place? Even these details don't tell us why this person is the main character in your song. What happened? Is the person still in your life? If not, where did she go and what were the circumstances of her departure? Did it hurt you when she left? Do you still miss her? If she is still in your life, what has changed since the time you remember? All these questions are really the same question in relation to your song. What feelings have been evoked by the sight of this stranger in the window? And what do your feelings mean to you? What do you care about in this story? When you add up all the details, the sequence of events, the physical environment, the sensory images, the names of your feelings, what happened or didn't happen, what is the ONE thing, the core idea that you are going to write a song about?

When real inspiration visits, there is no stopping it. There are few things more exciting to me than a new idea for a song, and several have come to me while out walking. When it begins to emerge, the feeling I have is very familiar, as if the song has been living in the ether, beyond my awareness, and now wants to be released. I know that if I harness the moment and capture the essence of the idea, I'm on my way. I also know that it may be weeks, months, or even years before the song is complete, but I know it's there waiting for me, calling me to pay attention to its voice, to really listen to its story, and to use my knowledge of craft, vocabulary, musical skills, and self-discipline to bring it into the world.

Another essential component in songwriting is telling the truth. I'm not referring here to the literal naming of names or reporting in chronological order a sequence of events (although that can be used in a song too). What's important is the intention of your song, the energy that drives it and belongs to you, is born out of your experience and insight. It is not contrived, attempting to be impressive, to be popular with an audience, or to sound like someone else. You should never have to ask yourself if you really mean what you are expressing, and this is sometimes harder than it sounds. I can't tell you how many times I have stumbled onto a phrase that sounded cool, a word that perfectly fit my rhyme scheme, or an exotic chord, only to realize that it wasn't what I really meant. It was inauthentic. So, I keep searching for something that is true. Even if your style of writing is fanciful and poetic, embellished with fictional characters and places, flourishes of cleverness, even completely invented details and descriptions, what you are representing, the underlying meaning, is your truth, your genuine thoughts and feelings. This approach is not just limited to the lyrics. Music can also be pretentious, or excessive, not serving the song. When all you hear is how flashy and sophisticated the changes are, how angular, nonintuitive, and hip the melody is, you may wonder if the composer really heard what was being written, or if it was merely an exercise in empty complexity, showing off (yes, I've done that too). Likewise, if the music is perfunctory and thrown together without imagination and care, it may shortchange an otherwise good lyric. A little more exploration of musical options, and commitment to going the distance, can bring the necessary energy to the words. In summary, go for the feels, tell the truth, and honor your inspiration with impeccable craft. Now let's get to work, telling the TRUTH about ONE thing.

Exercise 2: A Practical Process

Here is a songwriting process that may help you to begin writing if you are not sure what you want to write about. I use this method in my classes, and it's been successful in drawing out subject material that has energy. Remember, we're not about writing hit songs that adhere to a formula.

You'll see, when we get into the components of a song, there are many ways to stretch beyond the limits of common practice, and if you have an idea that gives you a buzz, if you have a substantial skill set, and the intention of following through to completion, you may write something exceptional. Please complete all the steps. I'm sure you will be glad you did. Here we go:

1. Make a list of 7 things that you are emotionally invested in. It may be a past or present lover, a cherished grandparent, an interesting stranger, a beloved place, a memory, an ideology, a political belief, a spiritual philosophy, an aspiration, an inanimate object, an animal, something that exists in nature, a conversation you remember, an event that broke your heart, or changed the course of your life, a small moment that created a large feeling within you, a scenario that became some part of who you are. The more personal your choices, the better. Follow the emotional charge of your topics. If you think of more than 7, keep writing your list, and use only a word or two to name each choice.

2. Select 3 things from your list. Choose the topics that are the most emotionally rich and personal to you. Now, write a couple of paragraphs of prose about each of these three topics. The goal is to mine as much as you can from each subject you have chosen, i.e., history, context, sensory details, and feelings that percolate around each one. You want to name aspects of your topics that light up the energy within you. Again, if you find that it takes more than two paragraphs, keep writing. What you write should enhance and intensify the feeling of being there inside of the subjects you have chosen from your list. If your writing doesn't trigger feelings, you might have to choose something else from your list. We're aiming for excitement, drama, juice, movement, attraction, vitality, laughter, tears, and most of all, meaning. You are starting with your personal point of view, and this belongs to you alone, so choose what you really care about.

3. Read your paragraphs aloud to yourself. Feel the impact of your words and read them again. Does one subject stand out more than others? Does one have a charge that gives you a brighter buzz than the others? Which one is truly worth the time and effort of writing a song about? Which one has the substance that feels closest to your own personal truth? Select one. Even if they all seem viable, now is the time to make a choice. Pick one. This will be the subject of your song.

4 You may want to continue writing prose about the subject you have chosen, and if you have more to say, keep going. But here is an important part of the process. Ask yourself this question: What is the ONE THING this song is about? This will be the unifying element that makes your song cohesive. Even if you end up with various tendrils and detours in describing what you want to say, don't lose sight of the one thing that is the core truth, the primary intention of your song. What is it? Write it down.

5 Create a working title. It's your song, and if you want to change the title somewhere down the road, you may do so. But for now, you are writing a new song and it's called: (whatever you decide to call it)

If you are already writing songs, this process may seem methodical. Your own approach may be more intuitive and spontaneous. If your method is meeting your needs, then you probably don't need this book. However, if you are reading this in hopes of expanding your process, and learning things you haven't tried before, you're in the right place. Consider the above exercise as the diving board. A few bounces and you will leap into many other aspects of songwriting. Along the way, you will fatten up your concepts and skills via your love of the subject you have chosen.

Expand Your Choices

Let's face it. The most predominant themes in popular music are driven by romantic love and lust. A few centuries ago, art was driven by religious worship, and the outstanding writers, composers, painters, sculptors of the times were writing about the deity of their chosen faith. In the 21st Century, the profane is more popular than the sacred, and we hear a lot of songs that mention body parts. When we follow the trends of commercial music, we may never get around to asking ourselves what we care about enough to commit to art. I do love a good love song, and the best of them can really touch the deeper levels of this nearly universal aspect of human existence. If the subject you have chosen to write about is in this category, try exploring some of the less obvious aspects of it, details that are unique to your own experience. I have written lots of love songs over the years, many forgettable, and a few exceptional. I also have a song called, "Elephants Walk to the Water" which describes exactly that scene and was written to convey my reverence for this magnificent beast. My song, "The Aerial View" describes what I imagined to be the impressions of life on Earth that aliens might form when they view us from space. I'm not an elephant or an alien, but I write about these things with feeling that is authentic for me. A few years ago, I was writing a musical theater piece with a friend of mine and wrote several songs from the point of view of characters in the story. The play never made it to the stage, but most of the songs are part of my current performance repertoire because they transcend the specific scenes from the play that inspired them. Life is so full of experience and meaning we can write about all kinds of things. There is an audience for intelligent, personal, artistic observation about anything that feeds the heart and the mind of the writer and the listener. Don't be afraid to write about subjects that are surprising and live beyond the narrow path of popular music.

Were you able to find a feeling-charged topic for your new song? Have you thoroughly explored the essence of it? Are you able to identify the ONE THING the song is about? Any subject that brings up powerful emotion may have several aspects that are meaningful to you. You don't have to write about all of them. Just pick one. A single idea, one that touches your heart and courses through your veins, is enough. Just pay attention. What stands in the center of your song? What else is in the room? Windows? Shadows? Kleenex for wiping away tears? Turn up your attention, focus, and write.

When I started writing songs, the bar was already pretty high. I was in my late teens when I first heard Laura Nyro and Joni Mitchell (young people who don't know these artists – do some research). I first fell in love with the courageous authenticity of emotion in their songs, expressed in freshly original musical approaches that drew from many influences. I knew for certain that both were writing about their real feelings, and people they really knew, things they did, places they had been to, and how they were touched by them. Both women were exceptional poets with bold imaginations, and both had a functional mastery of the instruments they played. They were creating beauty with all the elements of their songs – deeply personal and adventurous subject matter described in stunningly evocative lyrics, mysterious, surprising harmonic content, unaffected individuality in their vocal styles, melodies that used the entire vocal range, and song forms that were unpredictable. Both women were creating music that was downright cinematic in its range and impact. Both also took great care in arranging and orchestrating their music for recording, so that each album was a revelation.

Laura Nyro was writing surprisingly mature original songs when she was a teenager in New York City in the 1960s, songs she sang and played on the piano. Joni Mitchell was a Canadian folksinger who also played piano and found a signature guitar sound, working with open tunings. Both were recording albums of original material when they were in their early 20s. You can trace the trajectory of their early material through the years and hear their lives unfold, their truth, feelings and perspectives, their musical evolution, from youth to middle age. Each successive album was an education and we listened over the years as their musical skills and inspiration became more their own, and more musically sophisticated. Ultimately both accumulated a body of work that colored outside of the lines of popular songs and transcended the idea of "hits" (though each had songs that placed in the pop charts).

Each is now considered an artist, beyond the label of singer/songwriter. Although each achieved dazzling career highpoints, with broad critical acclaim, both eventually retreated from the spotlight. Laura Nyro died at the age of 49 in 1997. Joni Mitchell continued to record and evolve as both a musical artist and a painter, and received countless awards for her body of work before retiring due to health issues. Both women are still held in high esteem by anyone who aspires to reach beyond the popular trends in songwriting. Not only did both record numerous albums their fans still listen to tirelessly, but both have been honored by stellar tribute projects. Check out Herbie Hancock's tribute to Joni Mitchell called "River", and Billy Childs' album honoring Laura Nyro, "Map to the Treasure".

Tips

1. Listen to different kinds of music. Excellence can be found in every style and the acquisition of vocabulary will expand your songwriting ability. Fill your ears with unfamiliar sounds, classical to country, bebop to Brazilian, music from Mali and the Middle East. Listening with your full attention to music that is unfamiliar will open your ears to new ways of telling your story. Your lyrical ideas will be set to music and one of the many things you will decide is the musical personality of the song. Will it be a specific style or a hybrid blend of musical elements?

2. Keep a songwriting journal. Jot down any lyrical ideas that cross your mind. If a verse springs forth complete, grab it. Those of you fluent in musical notation should keep some manuscript paper nearby so you can write out a melodic idea. Most people carry smart phones that have voice recorders and notepad apps, so you don't have to forget your idea before you get home.

3. Listen to instrumental music. Classical and jazz are overflowing with emotional content and listening to the great composers in either genre may inspire ideas even though the music is wordless. I used to listen to the second movement of Beethoven's 7th Symphony and gaze out my window at the dark storm clouds in the Seattle sky, contemplating the mysterious force of this stately piece. When I was in high school, my art teacher used to play the Gil Evans/Miles Davis recording of Gershwin's Porgy and Bess in class while we worked. I loved it so much he gave me the album and I listened endlessly through the crackling scratches on the LP as feelings I couldn't name poured out of the grooves. Music speaks without words and ignites feelings that live beneath the surface. How might the work of another artist inspire your own songwriting process?

4. Characters in movies, books, magazine articles, or the news may also reach out to you and become the subject of your songs. When a story moves you and you can identify with the characters, what are the feelings that emerge? Does an iconic fictional character represent some part of your own psyche or circumstances? Can you empathize enough to write authentically, standing in the character's shoes (or your own shoes)?

For Example

I read a piece in New Yorker magazine about a young girl named Dawn who was living in challenging circumstances in the inner city. Despite her difficult life, she was determined to overcome the obstacles that might have beaten the will out of most people, and she did. I changed her name to "Birdy" and the song is in two parts – Birdy's world, and Birdy's dream. It's called "Silent City".

Birdy is a girl who lives in a room with nine other people
She sleeps on a sofa with the springs pokin' out
And the mice are eating through the wall
Someone's pissing in the hall
Birdy is a girl who lives in a room where the dirt on the windows
Steals the light and color from the day
Now it's the cryin' and the fightin' and the sirens and the traffic
And the stink and the hunger in the alley where the children play
From the shadows of the chaos she is watching the sky
And when nobody's looking little Birdy's gonna fly away

In Silent City the air is clean
And dawn brings the scent of the sea
I take my toast and honey on the balcony
Then bicycle down to the quay
Beautiful ladies in cotton dresses
Stroll with their babies, they're blowing kisses
And echoes of laughter like golden bells
On the shoes of a dancer

In Silent City a girl is free
The hours of the day are my own
When the sun falls rosy saffron down the lilac sea
The bicycle whispers me home
Counting the fireflies from the veranda
While sweethearts who pass by walk hand in hand
And the pearl light of moonrise is beckoning dreams
As the Earth sings a lullaby

Birdy is a girl who's reaching for the world
When nobody's looking, she will fly away

3
LYRICS

I have known many instrumental musician/composers who claim to never listen to the words of the songs. This is something akin to sacrilege for a songwriter. The lyrics tell the story of the song, and usually reveal the reason for writing it. Language is another facet of the artistic expression available in songwriting. Lyrics are something we care about and work hard to finesse. Instrumental tunes express moods, themes, and scenarios, and grooves, with a huge palette of sounds, and a full range of emotions, all without using a single word. But we are writing songs, and part of the definition of this musical expression refers to the vocal performance of it. Most vocal tunes include lyrics, and I listen to them as closely as I listen to the music.

Honesty

Subjective honesty is a powerful energy source in art. Creating music that is commercially viable for placements and sales is often the intent of songwriting courses designed for those seeking a financially lucrative career as a pro. But writing songs specifically with the intention of appealing to fans of popular music is not quite the same as the desire to look inward at what you as an artist, as an individual, want to express. Topics you truly care about may not be universal experiences or points of view and might have a limited audience. But a subject that is alive with meaning *for you* is enough to get you started. Rather than second guessing the population of mainstream listeners with attempts to create product that appeals to them, trust your own feelings and your own voice to express what's important to you. If you have chosen to follow an artistic path, you already know what's true and what's artifice in your writing. An artist with an original voice is not content copying familiar trends or filling the measures and beats with clever rhymes and catchy word combinations. What does your inner reality truly want to say? The resource of your own mind, your own experience, and your feelings is a well that never runs dry. People may love hearing what is true for you when your story is told in a great song. It may be true for them too.

Content and Method

I avoid making clear distinctions between the right way and wrong way to say what you mean. Some lyric writing methods are precise in their approach to structure, but my approach is less defined. Once I have an idea that has energy, I start writing. Words spill out, often on a napkin in a restaurant, on the back of an old receipt in my purse, or one of my many notebooks. They may unfold in the form of lyric phrases, or they might be more free flowing prose. An idea with a strong emotional essence will lead me to what I want to say. If you can speak and read, you are familiar with words, what they mean and what they sound like. A magic formula that always results in good writing does not exist.

Patterns we hear frequently in pop tunes, and the way they are taught, have been codified after the fact. Common practices in hit songs have first been observed and named, then offered to students as methods of approaching their own writing. I have not found these rules helpful, but many people swear by them. I'm more concerned with content than organizing syllables in terms of strong or weak emphasis. Listening to the way the words sound and knowing precisely what they mean has sufficed in my own writing. We should also remember that the songwriters we venerate probably didn't take songwriting courses or read books like this one. I care very much about good lyrics, but I never use a method of any kind other than the accumulated experience of listening to and singing great songs. I love the way words and music become a single unified thing in a song. I appreciate a good story told with fresh imagery and rhymes, subtlety, economy, cohesiveness, emotional depth, imagination, surprise, the musical sound of words, and truth. I also enjoy writing about my own observations and practices as a composer/lyricist, but like other teachers sometimes recommend, I advise you to take what you need from my approach and disregard the rest.

Rhythm in Words

When we are combining words with music, we must be aware of the rhythmic aspects of syllables. The consonants within a word can feel bright and percussive, while holding syllables for multiple beats combined with the sustained tones of the music emphasizes open vowels. Higher pitched notes that are held for a few beats tend to signal drama and intensity in the story. In the same way the notes in a melody can be subdivided into smaller increments, interspersed with rests, held for multiple beats, or placed in a syncopated relationship to the time, the syllables of words are also flexible and malleable. Their interaction with the musical beats and bar lines, in sync or contrapuntally, enhance interest and cohesiveness. When we are mindful of the rhythmic effect of the words, we can strengthen the rhythm of the entire song. We can create contrast by writing phrases that are active with many percussive syllables over a simpler rhythm in the music, or hold sustained vowel sounds over a rhythmically active musical accompaniment. If we have a problem fitting lyrical content into our musical structures, we can change the words or the melody so they feel connected. The term for a balanced and complementary relationship among all the elements of a song, like lyrics and music, is **prosody**.

Here is a portion of a song called "In a Perfect World". The groove is a medium uptempo funk shuffle, and my intention here was to choose percussive sounding words to fit the rhythmic feel of the music:

Everyone's got a daydream a fantasy
Everyone's got a somebody else they'd rather be
Running around, look at our friends, look at ourselves
We're going crazy
Everyone's got a nightmare a scary thing under the bed
The little voice of a memory, I don't wanna be
Alone in the dark sayin' a prayer, is somebody there
Gonna save me?

But someday everybody's gonna stand still
They're gonna stop screamin' and stand real still
And the silence all around
Is a wonderful sound
In a perfect world
In a perfect world
In a perfectly imperfect world.

Sensory Imagery

Memorable lyrics usually contain sensory imagery. Describing a scene with visual, aural, tactile, and olfactory references, literally or metaphorically, puts the listener there in the story. Telling a story without them is an option, but I'm a big fan of these images in lyrics. The scent of jasmine or smoke, the bracing wind, the sound of rain, the torpor or sensuality of heat, the play of the light at a certain time of day, the texture of skin, or the shade of blue in the sky, all bring vivid interest to the idea you want to relate. An old, abandoned building, a path deep in the woods, or a balcony overlooking the sea can set the stage. Using someone's name, real or invented, brings the character to life. Search your imagination for details like the coat someone was wearing, a theater program left on a café table, smells you notice driving through the desert at night, or walking on a city street early in the morning. They illustrate the feelings and faces associated with them. The choices you make can also create contrast as you describe the absence of a beloved person. Burt Bacharach and Hal David wrote a song called "A House Is Not a Home" and it describes the heartbreaking emptiness of a home when someone important has left. If your story is about a deeply emotional topic, search your memory for sensory imagery that gives atmosphere and a setting to your inner reality. You can say that you love food. Or you can say that you remember the blackberry pie that your Aunt Ruth brought to the picnic the summer if 1978. That image may lead you to reminisce about the carefree summers of long ago, or some special person who was there at the picnic, perhaps some unforgettable incident that occurred. Maybe that person became part of your life, or perhaps that person is a symbol of what has been lost with the passing years. Whatever the core intent is, it will be more impactful and dimensional when you bring it to life with your senses.

Here is a portion of an original song called "Song of the Bees". It is intended to evoke a memory of first love, from a long time in the past.:

How well I remember you standing so tall in the sunlight
Hair all a-tumble
Eyes whispering, "I'll see you there in the meadow
'Neath the apples trees"
The tender petals snowing down where we lay
In the wild grass
The song of the bees
Mesmerizing

Everywhere the air was sweet with clover
Everything was green and young and new
I could hear them as he won me over
Making love to everything that bloomed

How well I remember the scent of your sleeve as you held me
Arms like a river
Hands telling me, "I heard your name. I want your secrets.
Give them all to me"
A velvet song played all around where we lay
In the wild grass
The Song of the Bees
Hypnotizing

Everywhere the fevered air was buzzing
Lips like honey melting on my skin
The blossoms and the bees were lost to loving
The dance before the rapture and the sting

Nouns and Adjectives

You may have gathered by now that we are all about bringing our stories to life. This can be achieved in a variety of ways, but specificity is a big factor in giving the listener a mental picture of what you are singing about. A nonspecific noun might be a word like "tree". If you replace that word with a specific kind of tree – oak, pine, madrona, aspen, etc., we can see it in our mind's eye. If there is a vehicle in your story, what kind it? A van? A truck? A convertible? If your story includes a person, how about using a name? A little boy might be Joey, or a young woman could be Emily (not necessarily the name of a real person). If you're writing about a building, is it a bank, a store, or a house? Adjectives narrow it down even more – a twisted oak, a red Chevy with fins, little wild Joey, a faded ramshackle house. We're not writing prose here, so aim for balance between animating our story with specifics and being economical enough to fit your ideas into the framework of song lyrics. A detailed story can be captivating if the music allows it to flow without feeling forced. But if you need to trim away the extras in the interest of flow, be selective about which nouns and adjectives are the most important characters or objects in the whole scenario you are creating.

Verbs and Adverbs

Action words are another element that animates a story. Somebody *did* something and it moved the story from here to there. You could write: she said. Or you could write: she whispered, she cried, she barked, she snapped, she crooned, she revealed, she hissed, she reflected, she declared. You get it. How about adverbs? She fervently whispered, she seductively whispered, she shyly whispered, she discreetly whispered, she fiercely whispered, she gently whispered. "Whisper" is a musical sounding word and combining it with an adverb that also has appealing consonant and vowel combinations not only develops the image but adds to the flowing sound of the words in the context of the melody. If you think you might be getting too wordy, trust your ear to tell you if the balance is right. And as with all the descriptions you include in your songs, be aware of the sounds of the words and their rhythmic interaction with your groove. An inspired image may work beautifully in poetry or prose but feel clunky and forced in a song. If you're having trouble fitting it all in, you can adjust your music by making your phrases longer, subdividing your beats into smaller increments, or trimming away excess.

Actual Feelings

How literal should you be in describing your feelings? Some songwriters prefer to name the specific feelings they are writing about, but you can say so much without ever spelling it out. Sometimes the emotion is so apparent in the imagery you choose that you don't even need to name or express it directly. My own preference is the "less is more" approach. An occasional flicker of self-disclosure will ensure that your topic is not mistaken for something else, but you don't have to belabor phrases like, "I feel so alone", "I'm falling in love with you", "Why did you leave me?", or even the upbeat feelings like, "I feel so happy" (exception: Pharrell Williams, who has a lifetime pass to sing about happiness). Let your descriptions and impressions tell the story, while saving the naming of your feelings for moments of punctuation. Which is more evocative – *crying my eyes out*, or *tears falling like night rain against a smoke-stained window*? There is a place for a direct statement of feeling but placing it in the context of sensory imagery can make it real. *"First Time Ever I Saw Your Face"*, written by Ewen McColl and sung by Roberta Flack, is a tender and mesmerizing love song that describes the experience of falling in love without ever literally mentioning falling in love. The lyrical images and the music evoke the intention unmistakably. Bonnie Raitt sang a song written by Mike Reid and Allan Shamblin called *"I Can't Make You Love Me"*. The title is also the line that repeats in the chorus, but the set-up is a devastating scene perfectly described in a way that anyone can recognize. By the time she sings the chorus, we're already on the floor. This is one of the saddest and truest ballads of the 21st Century. For the sake of contrast, let's look at a tune written by Bruno Mars and Bhasker Jeffery called *"Uptown Funk"*. The blast of impressionistic imagery and groove in the song is a paean to having fun, releasing inhibitions, and giving in to the seductive joy of night life in the city. The intention of the song is clear without ever actually naming it. A ballad I used to sing in my jazz club days is a standard called "These Foolish Things" (written by Strachey and Link), is a list of sensory images that create a devastating sense of nostalgia, and it still chokes me up. The selective choice of memories in each stanza tells the story.

To Rhyme or Not to Rhyme?

Vowel sounds and ending consonants are the basis of rhyming words. "Moon" and "June" are simple rhymes that, when placed at the end of two different phrases, will tie the lines together. If you want to use rhyming words that have more syllables, like "sophisticated" and "dedicated", you are elevating the complexity of your phrases in a manner that can either be appealing if they are sincere or contrived if you are trying too hard to be clever. Traditionally, a solid rhyme scheme adds to the strength of structure and finesse in a song. An imaginative original rhyme is a treasure. A cheap or forced rhyme can stand out as a loose end. If you're going to create a rhyme scheme in your song, go the distance and choose your rhyming words carefully. Sometimes you can't find a word that means what you intend and rhymes perfectly in the spot where it belongs. "Almost" rhyming is enough for a song. Words that have a similar lilt and matching vowel sounds can function perfectly well as rhyme in a song, especially if they are also placed in a rhythmic frame:

Moonlight kisses the leaves
You are there in the dream
Like the air next to me
No one says anything

You may want to put rhyming words at the end of every line, or every other line. You can also include internal rhyme (rhyming words that occur within a single phrase, not just at the end), like "At first the *light* was so *polite* like a whisper on my eyes." You can also extend a single rhyme scheme to occur in multiple stanzas. If you choose to bypass the common practice of using rhyme in your lyrics, do your phrases hold up in the context of the music? It may be a stretch because we are so used to hearing rhyme in songs, but if you take this route, let your ear tell you if your choice serves the overall cohesiveness of your song. If the form of the music is tight, you may not even notice that the lines don't rhyme.

Similes and Metaphors

I've said a lot about the importance of sensory imagery in song lyrics. Similes and metaphors are effective ways of describing things in a manner that doesn't literally spell them out. A simile says: this is *like* that. A metaphor says: this *is* that. There are many trite cliches that have been used repeatedly in the function of simile and metaphor, i.e., "*light as a feather*", or "*it's raining cats and dogs*". These familiar images are used frequently in conversation, but in a song we need to think a little harder about what we want to say and to explore the options of descriptive words. If you keep reverting to tired cliches, spend more time immersing yourself in the emotion you are trying to portray and let your imagination deliver something fresh and uncontrived. A tall order, to be sure, but worth it.

Simile: *The moon was like a feather falling slowly down the sky.*

Metaphor: *The crescent moon is a silver boat setting out for the Island of Dreams..*

Exercise 3: Complete the Following Sentences

Finish each sentence using appropriate similes and metaphors, and try to avoid the obvious:

1 The cat walked along the rooftop like a _____.
2 That sarcastic remark hit me like a _____.
3 Seeing her welcoming smile was a _____.
4 The human family around the globe is a _____.

Alliteration and Repetition

Some songwriters sense that starting syllables and stuffing sentences with a series of similar sounding starters is a successful scheme for sonic satisfaction, but I suspect such steps to surely spill into silliness. (Alliteration)

Repetition can be very effective. I avoid repeating the same incidental or descriptive words too many times and I can usually think of different words that mean the same thing. If I get stuck, I get out my trusty Thesaurus. However, deliberately repeating an essential theme word or phrase emphasizes the identification of your subject. Repetition is prevalent in pop tunes which often have dramatic anthem-like choruses that occur two or three times over the course of the song. But repeated words don't have to be delivered as high drama. You can use them for emphasis in more subtle ways, keeping in mind the value of balance. Pay attention and trust your ear to tell you when you've repeated something too many times. When you have doubts about what you've written, if it just doesn't sound right, it's probably not. Trim away the excess until you find the number of repetitions that create emphasis without falling into boredom.

Repetition in a chorus:

Sleep in the arms of the dreamlight
Now you can let go
You know when it's your time
And when it's your time you will know
You will know

Dream in the arms of the quiet blue
Now you can let go
You know when it's your time
And when it's your time you will know
You will know

Impressionism

Impressionistic writing seeks to capture a feeling or experience with images that aren't intended to be a literal depiction of facts or feelings. In this approach, the rules of grammar and the sequence of events is less important than a blurry snapshot-like impression of emotional content. Authenticity still matters, but the listener is invited to fill in the blanks and determine which images are actual reality and which are metaphorical, textural, or atmospheric. The Impressionist movement in painting featured the works of Renoir, Degas, and Monet (among others), and in music, the composers, Debussey, Ravel, and Satie are considered Impressionists. Sometimes when you see paintings or hear music that is considered impressionistic, it may bring up feelings you can't quite name. Strong images that are not necessarily tied together with verbs, or even a specific sequence, allow the listener to supply the thread that connects them. Writing in this manner can lead you into a cloud of inspiration that comes from a place way beneath the surface of your conscious awareness. When this feeling strikes, write down everything that comes to mind and don't worry about sorting it out until you have grabbed whatever you can from the moment. You can distill this energy and its many tendrils as you get serious about the business of crafting your ideas. When it works, you may be creating a hypnotic quality that is greater than the sum of its parts. "*Calling You*", a song written by Bob Telson for the movie, "Baghdad Café", is a hauntingly impressionistic song that draws you into its ether with a mood of longing, an aching past and unknown future. Who or what is calling and why? We don't need to know because we already recognize the feeling that rises from between the lines.

This original song uses impressionistic lyrics to express the contrast between dark chaos and the balance of light:

Black crow calling from the telephone wire
Ashes across the sky
Iridescent midnight, the remains of the fire
Is that murder I see in your eye, my friend
Murder I see in your eye

The divas are wailing, it's festive in the tomb
Ashes across the stage
The audience died sometime well before noon
But the opera continued to rage, my dear
The opera continues to rage

Ashes, ashes, soot and smoke
We didn't see it coming,
Should have known it was a joke
Ashes, ashes, cinder and grime
It's a sad and tender little crime, this life
But the light on the lilies is sublime

Simplicity

Lyrics can be simple. If what you have to say is concise and appropriate to your intention, economy may be the perfect approach. Maybe your musical context requires fewer words than a detailed story would. Simple lyrics that are also mundane might be shortchanging the music, or feel like a placeholder more than a true statement of feeling. But sometimes words are textural sounds and don't have to present great imagination or profound meaning to serve their musical purpose. The percussive quality of certain words has a rhythmic effect within a groove driven song. Sometimes a few essential words can convey the essence of what you intend without a lot of additional description or explanation. "Shower the People" is a beautiful song by James Taylor that conveys simply and directly the idea that we should tell the people we love that we love them. Even using syllables that aren't words can be part of a song, a detail that highlights the rest of the words with contrast. This may be preferable to the clutter of too many words when the music is the core energy source of the song.

Humor

Many great lyricists use humor in their songs. If you have a good sense of humor and can use it to convey your feelings, whether you are commenting on politics, or the absurdity of life, love, and hairstyles, go for it. You can write a song that is occasionally or entirely humorous, using satire as the means to convey your theme. Tom Lehrer was a popular songwriter when I was a kid in the 1950s. My dad loved his records and played them constantly and the four kids in my family knew all the words by heart. They still make me laugh. His clever ideas were brilliantly executed as he performed them at the piano. Several prominent contemporary songwriters use humor frequently, including Tom Waits, Bob Dylan, Paul Simon, Leonard Cohen, and Donald Fagen, to name a few. Dave Frishberg was well known to jazz fans for his satirical songs such as "*My Attorney Bernie*", and the classic, "*I'm Hip*", which made everyone ask themselves, "Is that me?" He was also a very fine jazz pianist who accompanied himself. Even a little taste of humor in a song can be savory seasoning to more serious content. How funny are you? We all think our jokes are hysterical, but do you want to risk making your audience groan? Though humor is very subjective, if you think you have the knack, take the leap. You'll know after playing your song for someone else if it flies.

The Sound of Words

Words ARE music. The sounds of the words and the way they flow together is a detail that matters to listeners, even if they are unaware of it. For instance, if a word ends in multiple consonants, and the word that follows it begins with multiple consonants, they might not roll off the tongue with ease within the musical context. If you have managed to say exactly what you mean, but the words sound clunky and lack grace and fluency, that's another detail to revise. Some words are better for using in an essay or a report than in a song. When you recite your lyrics without music, can you still feel the music in them? I fell in love with Brazilian music many years ago, and part of what I loved was the sound of the language, even when I didn't know what it meant. English can sound like that too. When you go for an abrasive edginess and angularity in your content, the rough edges in the sound of the words can reflect that. Not everything needs to sound "gorgeous". Lots of beautiful words that evoke beautiful things can be too much of a good thing.

Dynamic Sequence

We have all read enough stories and novels to understand a sequence of events. Dynamics allow for the intensity to build from the beginning of the song to a moment when the meaning of the song is revealed, or the punchline is delivered. You can lay the groundwork for your destination by starting with a set-up, a "once upon a time" scene which introduces the story. You begin with a "before" and contrast it with the "after". First, I was feeling that way, then something happened, and now I feel this way. In a song about a deeply felt emotion, positive or negative, what is the origin of the feeling? How did you feel before? What changed? How do you feel now? If the song is about a single momentary feeling, some movement will be more interesting than static repetition. The density of the lyrics is another contrasting factor. Verses tend to be wordy, while choruses are more distilled. Your song may not have a verse/chorus form, so things like contrast and escalating degrees of intensity in your words can combine with the dynamics of the music to give movement to your themes.

Here is another excerpt from an original song that depicts a dynamic time sequence:

You're hiding from the racket, all the riot and the drone
You can't stand people talking but your heart was never meant to live alone
The winter sky was heavy, all the ash and rain so dark and low
But the city blooms like jasmine and the air is sweet when April breezes blow

Open up the window let that butterfly into your room
Send a message on her wings to the one who's waiting for you
Right outside your window is a butterfly with newborn wings
Looking for a garden where the columbine is waking up to spring
Mariposa, Mariposa, you never know when you might find love

Visit the Masters

Reading and studying the lyrics of songs you love is a way to acquaint yourself with the countless ways you can approach your own writing. Some of the songs I love have tightly crafted rhymes and rhythms, but some writers don't follow templates at all. Many of my favorite songwriters have been successful in making up their own rules. I'm going to list a few songs here, and if you are unfamiliar with them, *please find the recordings and lyrics online and check them out*. These are my personal choices, among hundreds of other songs I love, that offer examples of various approaches to using rhyme and rhythm, imagery, and emotion in lyric writing:

1. *"America"* is one of my favorite songs by Paul Simon. It's from the Simon and Garfunkel album, "Bookends", released in 1968. As complete and satisfying as the song is, the lines don't rhyme, and the song is not laden with obvious metaphor. Every phrase in the song is imbued with vivid imagery, and the story unfolds as a sequence of events. Did it really happen just like this, or is the whole thing a metaphor? Was Kathy a real person, or an invented character? It doesn't matter. The deeper meaning, the portrait of these two young travelers setting out on the journey of life into the enormity of the country is captivating, set to a wistful 3/4 time signature. The story is so engaging, we never wonder why it doesn't rhyme. The bridge is not only without rhyming words, but is also asymmetrical, and trails off in an implied ellipsis before the final stanzas and the drama of the crescendo and fade ending. Simply returning to the word, "America" at the end of each stanza is thread strong enough to hold the lyric together, without leaving us with any sense that something is missing

2. *"Make You Feel My Love"*, written by Bob Dylan in 1997 for his album "Time Out of Mind", is a ballad that expresses authentic feeling with a beautifully crafted symmetry. The words at the end of each line rhyme perfectly, and the rhythm of the phrases lines up with precision and ease. Unlike so many of Dylan's songs, there is nothing cryptic or elusive about the meaning of the song. The writing, his sincere declaration, is inspired enough to rise above the thoughtless emptiness of so many prefab pop love songs. The repeated lyrical motif, (when this or that bad thing happens, I'll be there for you), is said in a variety of ways, poetic, earthy, and passionate. Dylan has placed several songs in the pop

music charts over the years, and this song was recorded by more than 400 artists, including Adele, who had a huge hit with it. I teach it to all my singing students, arranged it for my chorus, and have sung it myself alone at the piano countless times. The lyric touches me every time.

3 *"We Belong Together"*, is a song penned by Rickie Lee Jones, and was the opening track on her 1981 release, "Pirates". It's also a love song of sorts, but the lyric is more dimensional and impressionistic than Dylan's hit. She does some imaginative things rhythmically, both in the shifting time feel of the music, and the placement of the words. Within the well-defined rhythmic framework of the song, she somehow manages to place far more syllables in every line than it seems there is room for, deftly making the edgy complexity fit within the bar lines. The effect is a cascade of pictures delivered in a flurry of consonants and syllables, dramatic and beautiful. The time and place she sings about overflow with the sad tenderness she feels for these characters. I consider this song Rickie Lee's masterpiece.

4 *"As"* is probably my favorite song by Stevie Wonder. It's a powerful tune, both brightly energetic and darkly driving in its intensity. The subject is devotion and true love, stating that no matter what happens, if the world becomes unrecognizable, if reason is no longer reliable, I will still love you. It's full of a zillion syllables and images, all delivered in an infectious uptempo groove. The music would stand alone even if the lyrics weren't so compelling, typical of Stevie's gift for melody. The verses, written in a major key with a very cool jazz-informed chord progression, are a perfect path that leads to a destination chorus in a minor key, insistent and chantlike. Stevie was always a master vocalist and he invests this song with such passion and robust elation that you can almost imagine a stadium full of people getting up and dancing together. Part of the magic here is that his choice of words is bold and original, and the lyrics have a strong percussive quality that interacts with the rhythm of the music. The dynamic trajectory, from the sweetness of the opening verse to the thunderous release of the repeated chorus at the end, is brilliant. The song is over 7 minutes long, but when I listen to it, I never want it to end.

5 *"You Must Believe in Spring"* is a stunning piece of collaboration in songwriting. The music was composed by Michel Legrand, and the

lyrics were written by the stellar team of Marilyn and Alan Bergman. Many of the standards that were written in the 1960s and beyond feature the exceptional lyrics of this prolific couple. Their style is one of elegance and impeccable craft and their work is the perfect match to many of the sophisticated songs that have become part of the contemporary vocal jazz repertoire. The song mentioned here has a reflective quality and offers one delicate image after the other, affirming the necessity of keeping hope alive amid a turbulent world, as is summed up perfectly in the title. The music is a complex composition and many instrumentalists have recorded it without lyrics. But the words have made it a vehicle for expressively deep singing, and it's been recorded countless times by many vocalists, including Barbra Streisand, Cleo Laine, and Sheila Jordan. But my vote for the definitive version is the duo recording by Bill Evans and Tony Bennett. There is a naked vulnerability in their rendition, two seasoned masters who have seen it all, done it all, and are now in the years of waning success. Bill Evans died not long after making this recording, but Tony went on to enjoy a huge revival of his career in the 1990s. For most jazz musicians the two volumes of duets these artists recorded together are a measure of musical excellence and sublime enjoyment. This song is one that stands out in the collection.

Exercise 4: Analysis of Lyrics You Love

Reading lyrics without the music makes me enjoy the song more when I hear it. I marvel at the art and craft some of my favorite songwriters bring to their lyrics. Choose a song with excellent lyrics. It can be a song that doesn't rock your world musically, but the lyrics should be special enough to you that when you read them aloud (without the music) you feel moved by them. Here you go:

1 Write out or type the lyrics so you can hold them in your hand and read them aloud to yourself several times. Don't just read them silently, but instead allow yourself to hear the words as you speak them.

2 What is the song about? Is it overtly stated or set into poetic imagery that doesn't hit you over the head. See if you can succinctly name the ONE THING the song is about.

3. Who is telling the story. Is it told in first, second, or third person?
4. Describe the storyteller. Include details that aren't mentioned in the song.
5. What is the emotional tone of the words, i.e., joy, grief, peace, anger, etc.
6. Can you name a sequence of events, a beginning, middle, and end? Or is it a mood song that depicts the emotional response to a snapshot situation?
7. Does it use rhyme? Can you identify the rhyme scheme?
8. What are some of the devices mentioned in this chapter the writer has included? Simile and metaphor? Humor? Impressionism? Rhythmic effects? Etc.
9. How do the words sound when you read them, apart from the content of their meaning? Is there a musical flow to the vowels and consonants in relation to each other?
10. Pull out a few phrases you find particularly well-crafted or moving. Why do you like them?
11. What about the musical setting of the lyrics? Is it equal to words in its ability to express emotion? Do the words outweigh the music, is the music the stronger element? Are they equal in impact?
12. Is there anything in these lyrics that you don't like? What might you have done differently?

How does all of this apply to you? Remember those paragraphs you wrote? Now is the time to read your favorite one again and begin to pull phrases out of it that will become the lyrics to your next song. This may be a long process, turning prose into verse, finding rhyme and structure that will become part of the whole piece of music. This is often the part of songwriting that becomes a little laborious for me. My notebooks are full of revisions, attempts that are crossed out, rewritten, discarded altogether, started anew, and finally settled upon as my working lyrics. I know that when I add music to the recipe, it might all change again. A good song is worth the effort. Start playing around with what you already have and see where it leads you. You may decide you're not interested anymore in your original idea and you want to start over. Or maybe parts of what you have written are solid, but some of it is expendable. It's your song, your lyrics, and your process, so you make the decisions about where it's going. Trust your intuition and preferences and try to ignore the yammering of the critical audience in your head. The students who take my classes bring their work to share with each other, and the feedback can be helpful. I always offer my honest opinion of their writing (with their permission), but defer to their choices, even if they are different from what I might have done. We are trying to establish some confidence in our own creativity, so practice listening to your lyrics from the inside instead of second guessing what your fans (or teachers) might want to hear. It's wonderful when a song begins to take on a life of its own and shows you where you are going with it. Just listen for the next words and notes to emerge and remember that the emotion you are writing about is the centerpiece of the song.

Folk music was a trend in the late 50s and early 60s and ran on a parallel track to the popular love songs on the radio. My parents listened to The Weavers, The Kingston Trio, and the Highwaymen. These artists performed traditional and contemporary folk music, usually with vocal harmonies and guitar accompaniment. Most college campuses had coffeehouses and folk clubs nearby where the music was performed, and as the country faced the turmoil of the Vietnam War and the Civil Rights movement, younger musicians were beginning to write songs of social and political commentary. A young man by the name of Robert Zimmerman, who lived in Hibbing, Minnesota, was inspired by the music of Woodie Guthrie and Pete Seeger, especially the compassionate observations of the struggles of working people. He worked on his own songwriting and went to New York City to hone his performance chops and polish his persona. When he returned to Hibbing, he had changed his name to Bob Dylan, and the folks back home knew he was a star in the making.

As the folk scene gained traction, Dylan's music infiltrated the pop scene with a genre called folk rock. Several bands had discovered Dylan's songs, his intriguingly cryptic lyrics set to acoustic guitar accompaniment, and before long they were adding bass, drums, and electric guitars to their arrangements of his material. Even Dylan himself began playing with a rock band, causing pandemonium in the folk scene where rock instrumentation was sacrilege. For a young guitar playing folkie like myself, it was a thrilling shift in the music we heard on Top 40 radio. Suddenly, lyrics meant something. The style expanded and morphed into a musical renaissance bringing forth the stunning songwriting of troubadours Crosby Stills and Nash, Judy Collins, Joni Mitchell, Donovan, Leonard Cohen, Laura Nyro, and James Taylor. Even the Beatles, the most popular band of all time, admired and were influenced by Dylan. While these artists developed their own original voices, Bob Dylan was the songwriter who turned the tide and persuaded mainstream audiences to appreciate lyrics that were equal to the music, and sometimes surpassed it. These artists demonstrated how an original and finely tuned lyric could reach beyond the trite phrases and worn out cliches of teen love songs – and sell records.

Countless great songs have been written and recorded in the decades since Dylan first arrived on the scene. People aren't buying CDs like they once did, but something I always enjoyed was reading the lyrics to the songs printed on an album cover or a CD insert. Reading them separately from the context of the song, could be a completely satisfying experience. When the music was also inspired and well crafted, popular music was elevated to the level of artistry. Here are a few more names of exceptional lyricist/composers who have made *an impression on me: Rickie Lee Jones, Tom Waits, Donald Fagen, Randy Newman, Paul McCartney, Paul Simon, Tracy Chapman, and Sting.*

I want to also mention my favorite lyricists of the Tin Pan Alley years. It was a different time then culturally and the popular music of the day was often featured in movies and plays. Songs were romantic, sometimes frivolous, but these melodies and lyrics have remained popular, and this repertoire became the centerpiece of vocal jazz. I have enjoyed singing many of them and I have a few favorite lyricists: Dorothy Fields, Yip Harburg, and Johnny Mercer worked with numerous composers during the years when songs were often written by composer/lyricist teams. Hal David was the other half of Burt Bacharach's hits in the 60s and 70s, and Marilyn and Alan Bergman wrote lyrics for many contemporary standards. Two exceptions to this collaborative approach in the second quarter of the 20th Century were Cole Porter and Irving Berlin, who each wrote music and lyrics, and some of their songs were among the best of the standards. Stephen Sondheim started out collaborating with Leonard Bernstein in the songs from "West Side Story" but went on to write words and music to dozens of beautiful songs that appeared in Broadway musicals. Several of his songs have become part of standard jazz and cabaret repertoire

Tips

1. You should own a Dictionary, a Rhyming Dictionary, and a Thesaurus. I use them all frequently. If I have any question about the meaning of a word, I check it in the dictionary. A rhyming dictionary is a last resort when I just can't think of that one rhyming word I need. Of course, in a list of words that rhyme, you must find one that means what you want it to mean. A Thesaurus, a collection of words that mean the same thing, is a great resource if you find yourself using the same word too many times.

2. A novelist friend of mine helped me out once when I was stuck and unable to move forward with a lyric. He introduced me to the idea of "inside out, outside in". What that means is to write a balance of internal emotional description and external sensory imagery. That simple concept saved my song, which was full of imagery, but I needed to be more specific about the feelings I was describing.

3. I love impressionistic writing, but in my own songs, I insist that everything I write means something and has a purpose. I don't necessarily want to explain what I mean, but I want to be able to. I write as honestly as I can from my perspective and avoid concocting an impressive smokescreen. When I know what I mean and have put it to the authenticity test, I don't mind if my audience doesn't understand the literal meaning of my song. When James Taylor was asked about the meaning of his lyrics, his reply was (paraphrased), "If I wanted to spell it out, I wouldn't have written it in a song".

4. Ask yourself again: What is the ONE thing my song is about? Is it true? If you start meandering in your lyrics, check in with what your original intention was. You may have to nudge yourself back onto the path of your destination, and ask yourself, did I really mean that, do I know it's true for me?

5. The mind is a wonderful thing. If you need that perfect rhyming or descriptive word, the perfect flow of syllables and sounds, but can't seem to pin it down – ask your mind to help you. When I'm stuck I say, "okay, mind, give me what I need", then I put down my pencil and walk away from the piano. Very often, especially after sleeping on it, the very words I was looking for come to me like a download. Miracle? Nah, it's just how the mind works, (which is pretty miraculous).

The next few chapters deal with the musical part of songwriting. I have included some specifics about music theory in relation to each topic. The most fundamental elements of theory are indicated (**TA** – Theory Alert) and are printed in italics so that readers who already understand the material can skip over it. The chapters also contain my own subjective thoughts on the various aspects of theory and how I have approached them in my own writing. These may be of value even if you are already fluent in theory.

I often suggest that you trust your ears in making musical choices. I want to encourage you to decide for yourself if you really like what you are creating. You can write music and be impeccably correct but still miss the gratifying experience of loving what it sounds like. You may stumble upon beauty by accident or design, but you are the one who decides. If what you are writing feels perfunctory, trust that perception too and keep exploring.

4
MELODY

A series of consecutive pitches can be arranged in what seems like an infinite number of ways, and if you include time values and rests, even more combinations are available. If we narrow that down to notes sung by the human voice, the choices are fewer, but still allow for more combinations than most of us will think of in our musical lives. As singers, we are all about melody. It's an essential element in songwriting and is usually where the lyrics live. As a single note instrument, the voice is called upon to hear and reproduce the correct notes, without buttons, keys, or frets to give us tactile reinforcement. The brain formulates a pitch, the vocal folds respond with the right length, density, and rate of vibration as the air moves through them causing the sound vibrations to resonate in the head. From thought to sound, it takes only a split second. It's a miraculous mechanism and when we use it to sing, the voice can deliver a complex sequence of notes and lyrics in intricate combinations of sounds that tell a story – hands free. As singers, we love a good melody. As songwriters, let's write them.

Default Melody

Popular songs in the 21st century are usually melodically simple. Melodies in hit songs often seem to be composed by pulling out a few prominent notes from the simple chordal accompaniment and following it through a limited number of chords as they change. I have worked with students who wrote songs by downloading from the Internet sequences of chords in 4 bar repeated patterns. The melodies they create are passable within the abbreviated framework, but without a fully composed chord progression, the repetition can feel static and dull. If you accompany yourself on guitar or piano, you can unwittingly lock your melodic concept into a path-of-least-resistance approach. Your melody notes may only consist of the upper voices of the chords you are playing without the additional use of consonant scale tones. This is especially monotonous if you are playing a repetitive progression in one key without any harmonic movement. Rhythmically speaking, you may be so tied to your comping pattern you are not allowing your melody any rhythmic independence. You may stumble onto something minimally workable and not realize you could have made more imaginative choices. Occasionally a song is great even without an intentionally constructed melody. I was in the grocery store the other day and they were playing "Sweet Dreams are Made of This" by Annie Lennox. Loud. The entire melody is a repeat of about four notes and a few chords. Like the other shoppers, I was singing along and all I could think was, "What a badass tune!!". The groove is irresistible and the killer performance by Lennox doesn't let up for a second. Nevertheless, while melodies don't have to be expansive and complex to serve the purpose of the song, when you consider what the possibilities are, are you just scratching the surface of good melodic writing? Don't opt for simplicity because you don't have the initiative to push through the most obvious options to something more interesting. Current trends in popular music will teach you to do more of what is already being done. When you imitate these styles, it's fairly easy to replicate the hits that you are listening to, but if you want to evolve your songwriting to include all the elements of music, your creativity will not be limited to imitation.

Melody Rich Music

I've had some experience singing classical music and jazz, both of which I loved. Melody is prominent in these styles and essential to the currency of the music. Classical singing is challenging. The exceptional vocal range and impeccable musicianship required to sing this music can be discouraging for all but the most talented and dedicated singers. Nevertheless, it's fun to pretend as you soar through the delicious melodies of Puccini (my favorite). The standards, the heart of American vocal jazz repertoire, composed between the 1920s and early 60s, are very melodic songs. The song forms were somewhat limited, but melody was not. I first heard my mother singing them while she was ironing. She had a clear voice and great intonation, and she sounded to me like the singers on the radio. Studying jazz requires a focused dive into the intricacies of the relationship between the melodies and the chord progressions of these little masterpieces. Learn to sing and play fifty standards in several keys and not only will you understand basic harmonic theory, but your melodic vocabulary will also be vastly elevated. The composers of the time, Gershwin, Kern, Porter, Berlin, Carmichael, Arlen, and so many more, wrote brilliantly elegant melodies, some simple but many quite complex, balancing art and craft. Many of the more contemporary jazz composers have written melodies that are equally creative and beautiful. Some of these modern melodies can seem somewhat eccentric and difficult to sing, but many are worth the challenge of learning them.

TA: Scale Degrees and Chords

Much of Western (not cowboy) music is comprised of the notes of the major scale and its relative minor scale. That may seem like a very broad statement but a great deal can be done with these tonal components, combining and modifying them in countless ways to create melody. There are other systems of scale tones, but the major scale (and its relative minor) is by far the most commonly used in Europe, North America, and South America. It is comprised of a series of whole steps and half steps that maintain their relationship to each other regardless of what key they are in. The basic formula for the major scale is the 7 tones plus octave, with half steps between the 3rd and 4th degrees, and the 7th and 8th degrees. The relative minor has the same key signature as the major scale but starts on the 6th degree of the scale and consists of the 7 consecutive tones that follow it. When you move the tonic (starting note) of the major scale to the 6th degree of the scale, the placement of half step intervals moves to the 2nd and 3rd degrees and 5th and 6th degrees, and the scale now contains a minor 3rd. If you are not familiar with how this sounds, please get yourself a beginner piano book and go to a piano and play these scales. You can start a major scale or relative minor scale on any pitch and the melody will sound the same if you use the same formula of whole steps and half steps, but as soon as you leave the key of C on the piano, you will be introducing sharps and flats (black keys) to keep the whole step/half step sequence intact.

Check out the graphic illustration of the piano keyboard below for a clear idea of whole steps, half steps, and how relative major and minor keys are tonally connected. When you play these scales on the piano, start by learning to identify by ear the difference between a whole step and a half step. Half steps are the relationship between every adjacent key, black or white. C to C# is a half step. Whole steps are the relationship between every other key. C to D has a black key between them so they have an every-other-key relationship to each other. The same is true moving from E to F#. It's useful to be able to identify these relationships on the keyboard and the staff, but also very important to identify them by ear. You will only be able to do this by playing and singing them.

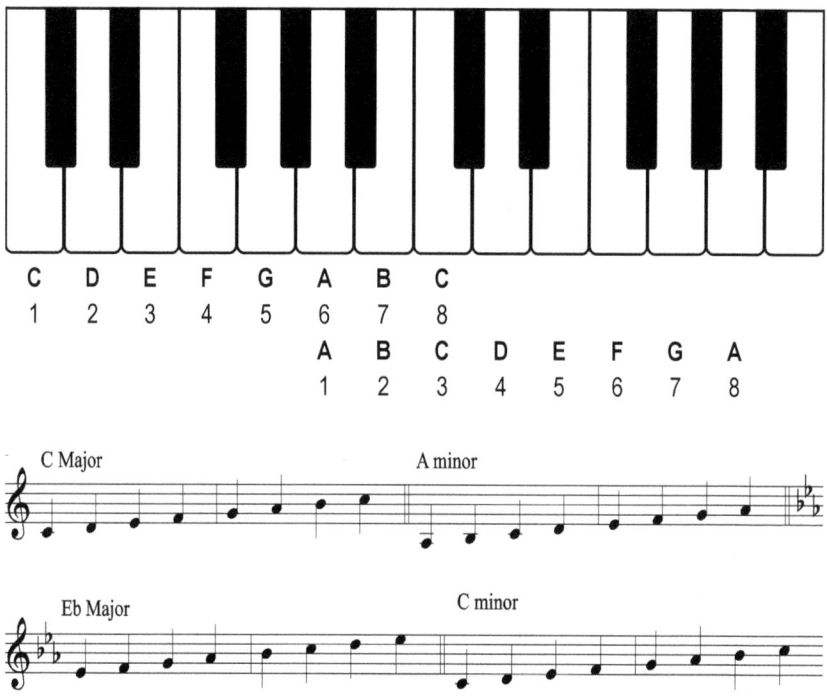

This book is not a source of complete instruction in music theory, but I want to mention something that isn't obvious to some songwriters. When you play a series of chords in sequence, you are likely (not always) implying a tonal center, also called a key, that has corresponding (consonant) scale tones. When you play a sequence of unmodified chords like: C – Am7 – Dm7 – G7, whose roots and chord tones are specific degrees of the C major scale, you are creating a tonal atmosphere that implies ALL the notes in C major. The chords played in this sequence create a **I vi ii V** (1-6-2-5) progression because the roots are on the first, sixth, second, and fifth degrees of the scale. A **I vi ii V** progression in the key of Eb would include the chords, Eb – Cm7 – Fm7 – Bb7, and when you see this group of chords together you know the consonant melody choices will be the notes of the Eb major scale. If you tend to only hear the prominent notes of a chord, like the highest pitched chord tone in the accompaniment, you might limit your melodic choices. Drawing from all the notes of the scale to craft your melody can be more expressive. In addition to specific scale tones, many other notes may be added to your melody while retaining the tonal center that identifies the key of your song. This is a very simplistic description of the process but is perhaps informative to those who don't know it. There are many combinations of chords and corresponding melodic choices, including minor chords and their scales. Tonal centers may also shift within one song, something you see frequently in jazz standards. When a song is written in a specific key, it may contain melody notes and chords that are not in that key, and in many styles of music, it is common to borrow notes and chords from another key rather than stay exclusively within one key.

Melodic Variations

Let's look at some possibilities in constructing melodies. A good melody may contain any or all the ideas on the following list, or things I haven't mentioned here. Your ears will tell you if your choices are musical within the context of your song. The following examples are melodies that are consonant with **C** major, or its relative minor, **A** minor, and are only taken from these scales:

1 Within the rhythmic and harmonic structure of your composition, a melody can repeat the same note over changing chords.

2. A simple chord progression offers the option of creating contrast with a complex melody. In relation to your time signature and tempo, try going for smaller increments of rhythm in your melody, i.e., 8th notes, 16th notes, or triplets, which can give a percussive feel to your phrases.

3. You may want to choose fewer notes of longer duration, like whole notes, or half notes. An interesting melody will usually contain combinations of long and short notes.

4. You might choose large interval jumps, stepwise motion, arpeggios, and ascending or descending lines.

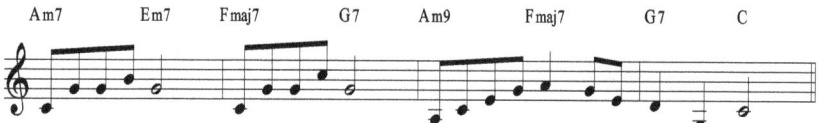

5. Syncopation is also an interesting melodic detail that comes from the rhythmic aspect of melody.

6. How about space? We have notes and we have rests. The silence between notes can be eloquent.

7   Pick-up phrases lead to destination notes, and chromatic detail can be a sophisticated touch.

Melodic Motif

Melodic motifs are short figures of note combinations that can be repeated and modified, to give a strong identity to your melody. The note cluster that comprises your motif can move in shape through different chords, modifying pitches to maintain consonance. They can also be shortened or elongated with varying time values. Motifs are featured prominently in Tin Pan Alley standards. Listen to "Somewhere Over the Rainbow" by Harold Arlen, and the more contemporary "Make You Feel My Love", by Bob Dylan.

Here is an example of a melodic motif:

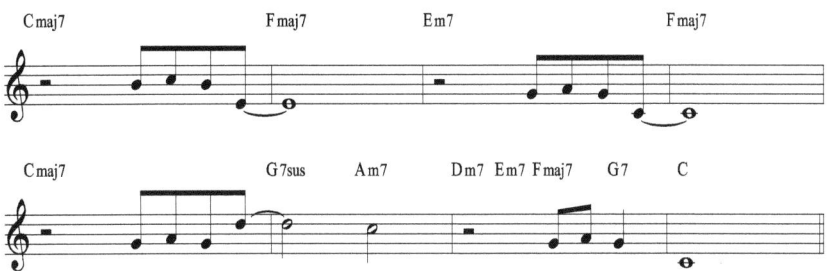

The Blues Scale

The sound of the blues scale is prevalent in popular music, especially the music of the African American culture. Much of the melody that is sung or played in a blues tune is derived from this group of notes. Blues melodies are often improvised, and additional notes may be added, but most of the content of the melody is built on this scale. While the major scale has 7 tones, the blues scale has 5 tones: 1 – b3 – 4 – 5 – b7. You will often also hear a b5 between the 4th and 5th. Blues melodies often consist of "licks", groupings of these notes that happen frequently. You will also hear the notes of the blues scale in the ornamental melismas sung frequently in R&B, rock, and soul music. "Blue" notes can be added to melodies derived from the major scale to give them a blues flavor. We'll look at the harmonic components of blues in the next chapter.

Singability

Melodies can be simple or complex but should flow in a singable way. It's fun to throw in some surprising notes, but they should feel musical in context. If you can sing the song accurately, in tune, unaccompanied, even if it's complicated, that's a sign of melodic strength. I wouldn't discourage going for a melodically challenging melody if you have the ears and the chops to pull it off. But if your melody is so far out you can't sing it in tune without accompaniment, it may not be that fun to listen to either. There are plenty of excellent songs that have difficult and complicated melodies, and they often take extra work to learn to sing them accurately. If you opt for melodic eccentricity, be sure you mean it. A student of mine once said, "Sometimes weird is good, and sometimes it's just weird".

Melodies without Chords

If you are not fluent on a chordal instrument, try finding a melody with your voice. But beware, unless you have impeccable pitch and memory, you may have trouble remembering what you sang. Often when singers show me their melodies unaccompanied, they are unable to stay grounded in their tonal centers. It's easy to meander all over the place and lose track of your harmonic context when you don't have the guidance of a chordal accompaniment. Writing out your melody on manuscript paper or recording it on your phone are options for keeping track of your ideas. It's a worthwhile investment of your time to learn to write out your music with tonal and rhythmic precision. Composing a melody unaccompanied might produce a beautiful result if you can document what you sing. If you already have lyrics, try singing them without an instrument in hand and see if your melodic ideas are a little freer than they are when you accompany yourself on piano or guitar. If you find something you like, add chords, keeping in mind the necessity for consonance between melody and harmony. You can always adjust anything you write if something is clashing in these relationships.

The Low and High of It

Think about dynamics. Tension and release are ideas that work throughout all the aspects of composition, and in melody this can be a set up that leads to the delivery of a prominent destination note. If the details of a story happen in the middle and lower range, high notes take us to a different part of the song, a punchline, a prominent emotional detail, something of stronger intensity than other parts of the melody. When your melody has taken you to a dynamic high point to punctuate an important moment in the story, you may then want to return to the middle or lower range to contrast the development of the details. This approach is also dependent upon your vocal range, but even a little variety of this type in your melody can add interest. When your melody sits in the middle of your range throughout your song, even if the melody varies, it can have a monotonous and static feel

Beyond Scale Tones: Many More Colors

The focus up to this point on major and relative minor scale tones as a source of melody is primarily to acquaint songwriters with the foundational principle of scale/key relationships. But this is a limited palette. There are many more ways to approach melody in a song by adding accidentals, sharps and flats that don't naturally occur within the scale. As harmonic accompaniment expands beyond scale tone chords by modifying the qualities of the chords, or modulating outside of the basic tonal center, many more notes are available to add to your melody. We'll look at this more closely in the next chapter, but here is an example of some harmonic/melodic modifications you might see in the key of C. This is more of an illustration than a song but play through it to hear what you're looking at. The roots of the chords are scale tones in C major but the qualities of some of the chords have been modified opening up more melodic choices:

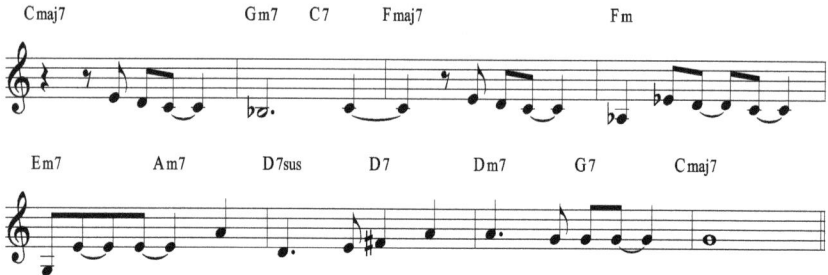

Exercise 5: Adding Melody to a Chord Progression

Compose melodies that are consonant with the following two 8-bar chord progressions. The first one is in the key of C major, and the notes of the C major scale will fit the chords. Your choices will include be the pitches of your melody, their relationship to each other, and the duration of each note or rest. For fun, write several melodies for each 8-bar progression.

The second group of 8 bars is in the key of Eb major, but takes a few detours out of the key, borrowing chords from other keys before returning to Eb. Again, determine the components of the chords, the tonal centers, and write a melody consonant with the progression.

The third progression is in D minor. Notice how different a minor melody feels from a major one. First play the D minor scale that is the relative minor of F major (hint: it has the same key signature as F major).

1

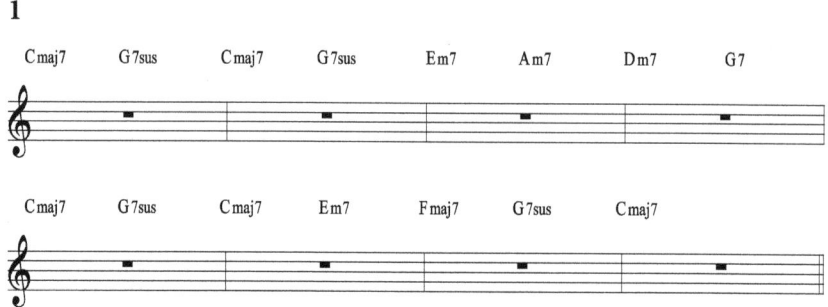

Now, let's get back to the song you started working on a few chapters ago. You have a working set of lyrics, so let's get going with a melody. I often find the process of writing melody to be very much informed by what is happening harmonically, but often the melody and harmony develop together. And sometimes the lyrics suggest a good melodic idea. I go with it and add the changes that fit my melody. The rhythmic nature of your lyrics will certainly influence your melody, and you can choose combinations that line up in sync, or contrast with each other. If your lyrics have a defined theme you can decide what kind of mood and tempo your song will be, even if you have yet to write melody and chords. Is it a dreamy ballad, or a punchy feel-good tune? We'll get into the finer details of harmony and rhythm in the coming chapters, and these elements will undoubtedly inspire your melodic choices. For now, read your lyrics again and see if any melodic ideas emerge. Be sure to write them down or record them

We learn so much about art and craft from studying and copying the masters who have gone before us. I became acquainted with jazz in my early 20s. My boyfriend at the time was a jazz guitarist, and he urged me to try singing the songs that Flora Purim recorded with pianist/composer, Chick Corea in the 1970s. I remember having to study them diligently to sing them with accuracy. I was always a nut for learning a melody correctly and some of the intervals in these songs did not come to me intuitively, so singing them was a major expansion of my ears. The jazz bug bit me, and as a fledgling vocalist in the San Francisco jazz scene, I was hearing things that challenged me and scared me. The tunes were unfamiliar, and so much more complex than what I was used to, but I soon developed a preference for music that was multidimensional and surprising.

In addition to the treasures of Tin Pan Alley, many tunes in the vocal jazz repertoire were originally composed and played by master instrumentalists. Later, when lyrics were added, singers enjoyed performing them too. Thelonious Monk was a truly original pianist/composer, with a signature quirkiness in his approach to melody. Carmen McRae recorded an album of Monk tunes in 1990, several of which featured lyrics by John Hendricks. Songs like "Reflections", "Ugly Beauty", and the more familiar "Round Midnight", are wonderful vehicles for vocal performance.

Billy Strayhorn, who often composed with Duke Ellington, was also a lyricist. His beautiful, world weary ballad, "Lush Life", is so sad it's almost hard to imagine Strayhorn writing this as a very young man whose life was just beginning. The melody is deep and challenging, and perfect for the story he was telling. He also composed the lovely "Daydream", and hypnotic "A Flower is a Lovesome Thing". He went the extra mile in crafting songs with lyrical, yet surprisingly complex melodies.

Bebop is another approach to jazz melody. Most often played at burning fast tempos, these melodies are full of chromatic detail, flurries of notes in every bar, and surprising zigs and zags. Charlie Parker was the prominent composer of this style (along with Dizzy Gillespie, Bud Powell, and Miles Davis, to name a few), and "The Omni Book" collection of his tunes and solos has found its way onto many a jazz musician's music stand. There are lyrics to several of his most popular tunes, and singers who perform them need advanced level chops to cover these finger-shaped melodies.

I first heard saxophonist Wayne Shorter's collaboration with Brazilian singer, Milton Nascimento, on an album called "Native Dancer" that was recorded in the 1970s. It was a masterpiece. The mysterious passion of the writing got under my skin, with melodies that were hard to sing, but stunning – especially in the Portuguese language. Shorter wrote many singable melodies, and this marriage of jazz and Brazilian music is one of my favorite albums of all time and was the gateway to my love of Brazilian music. Check out "Ana Maria", a melody so exquisite it still grabs me by the heart.

Contemporary jazz songwriters draw from everything that went before, i.e., standards, world music, funk, rock, classical, etc. As a songwriter with some background in jazz, and many other styles, I never think about what label to attach to my songs. Songwriters like Esperanza Spalding, Becca Stevens, Luciana Souza, Gregory Porter, and Jacob Collier are writing tunes that are extraordinarily beautiful and musically sophisticated. My brief list here is just a sample of what's out there that might expand your concept of melody. This feast of musical delights is so abundant, we'll never catch up with our listening.

Tips

1. Listen for the next note. When you sing part of a phrase and don't know where to go next, listen for it. You will likely find the exact pitch you're looking for, and you might find whole phrases this way. Your imagination will hand you things that are just right (this works with lyrics too)

2. If your attempt to make your melody interesting results in too many ideas, it will lose cohesiveness. A couple of strong themes with some dynamic contrast should create interest and balance. Too much going on, too many shifts and turns, too many surprises, can dilute the strength of your main idea. Save something for your next song.

3. When you repeat a melodic theme, find the number of repetitions that are meaningful without repeating it so frequently it becomes monotonous. No, there is not a fixed number that works, but your ears can tell you.

4. Music from non-western cultures often has mind blowing approaches to melody. Listen to some East Indian Raga, Klezmer, Vietnamese, Wassoulou, or Bulgarian music, for example. It's fascinating to hear melodies that emerge from different tonal vocabularies. I have heard some jazz singers incorporate East Indian melodic detail into performances of standards, for example, with surprisingly wonderful results.

5. When you write your lyrics first, you may opt for a meter and a regular number of syllables per line. Then, when you add your melody, it may have a boxy feel that matches the rhythm of the lyrics. Again, look out for too much repetition in a symmetrical melodic line. If all your lines have the same melodic and rhythmic shape, try using some variation so it feels like your story is going somewhere.

5
HARMONY

Pitches played consecutively create melody, while pitches played simultaneously create chords. The term "harmony" is often used to refer to the additional vocal parts that accompany a lead vocal. This isn't wrong, but for our purposes, harmony will refer to the chords in the song, their relationship to each other, to melody, to mood, and movement. Harmonic theory is a huge topic and again, I strongly suggest that if you aren't already fluent in this aspect of composition, do yourself a favor and study it.

If melody is the face of the song, harmony is the inner life. Harmonic progressions (groups of chords played in sequence) create much of the emotional content of the music. There are many types of music that traditionally contain only a handful of chords played in their most basic form, and some that don't use chords at all, but accompany the voice with instruments that create a drone. Folk, country, rock, blues, and other popular styles have gotten along just fine using 4 root position chords (sometimes referred to as "cowboy chords"), but when you begin to understand the range of choices in the realm of harmony, the skies open and the light pours in, along with all the rest of the weather. Chords can bring wondrous layers of meaning and depth to your melodies when you move out of cowboy territory and really begin to explore what's available. You should own a keyboard of some kind and have enough facility in reading music that you can match the notes to their lines and spaces on the staff. If you don't know this basic keyboard vocabulary, it will be easy to learn it, and of great benefit to your understanding of harmonic theory.

Chord Progressions

When most of the music you listen to is harmonically simple, you may not know what's possible. Popular music creates dynamic movement with lyrics, melody (to some degree), arrangement, and performance, but often neglects the range of available harmonic content. When chords are played in a specific sequence, they create a *chord progression*. The word "progression" is an accurate description of the way chords work together in a song because, like lyrics and melody, they move your story forward. The chord/melody relationship becomes a unified element of the music, i.e., chords suggest melody and melody suggests chords. Chords interacting with each other in sequence are part of the energy that animates and gives emotional depth, mood, subtext, and momentum to the song. The information and examples I share here will be useless unless you can play them and hear what they sound like. In the same way that the word "dragonfly" is not an actual dragonfly, words written about music, and even musical notation, are not music. Go to the piano and try out these examples so that you begin to develop an aural association between the symbols and the sounds. You don't need to be a pianist to use the piano as an instrument that will help you comprehend the concepts and sounds of theory. Learning the names of the keys, and the lines and spaces of the staff is a good place to start, and you can easily acquire a keyboard without a huge monetary investment. Consider it an essential educational tool that will lead to big rewards in your understanding of music.

TA: *Scale Tone Chords*

If what follows here sounds like word salad, you need to investigate a little further into the fundamentals of music theory. When you play a triad on each note of the major scale, the resulting chords will have their own basic qualities if they are unmodified. As you play these triads you will see that each chord contains either a major 3rd (two whole steps from the root of the chord) or a minor 3rd (one and a half steps from the root) depending on which scale degree is the root of the chord. This is because, as you move through the scale, the relationship of the scale's half steps and whole steps shifts. Without the addition of accidentals, the first, fourth, and fifth degree scale tone triads are major, while the second, third, sixth, and seventh scale tone triads are minor. This is always true unless you add accidentals to *change it – and that happens frequently. When the qualities of chords are changed with the use of accidentals, they may also functionally belong to a different tonal center, depending on the context of melody and surrounding chords. The chords that appear in the C major scale will also show up in other keys, but in a different order and context than they do in the key of C. In the unmodified context of the key of C major, these are the scale tone triads in the key of C and A minor:*

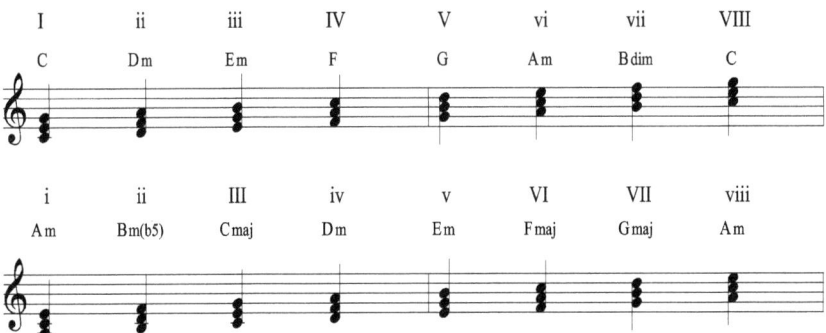

When your story needs a musical atmosphere that isn't satisfied with scale tone triads, you have many choices. Your ears may be drawn to sounds that are more loosely tethered to familiarity, and if you choose to explore harmonic territory that is more open, this will probably impact your melodic choices too. There are degrees of anarchy here and some harmonic conventions that once seemed edgy are now part of our daily aural landscape. When you start to play with alternate choices, listen to what other musicians have done and see if you can incorporate their explorations into your own musical vocabulary. There is no substitute for analyzing the harmonic structures of existing songs, and in particular the work of jazz composers. Expanding your ears will expand your choices. Let's see what's possible.

Chord Extensions

Your harmonic recipes will grow with the added flavors of chord extensions. Moving beyond basic triads and adding notes to any major, minor, or dominant chords can make a world of difference in the richness of the sound. If you are curious about how to expand your melodic vocabulary, invest in a few good jazz fakebooks. Most of the standards that have survived the many decades since they were first written have been modified with jazz chords. You will see chords that seem somewhat complicated, with additional information besides the letter name and basic quality you see in a scale tone triad. Although these chords function in ways that are similar to their simpler versions, they are often more interesting, and bring more dimension to the music. The chords below are called Scale Tone 7th Chords. By adding an additional note to a scale tone triad, you begin to hear the harmonic richness that is available to your expanded ears. Be aware that although it looks like these notes are stacked up on top of each other, in real music, the voicings of chords (order in which notes are played together) allow for the individual pitches to be spread out in a way that is more pleasing and balanced to the ear.

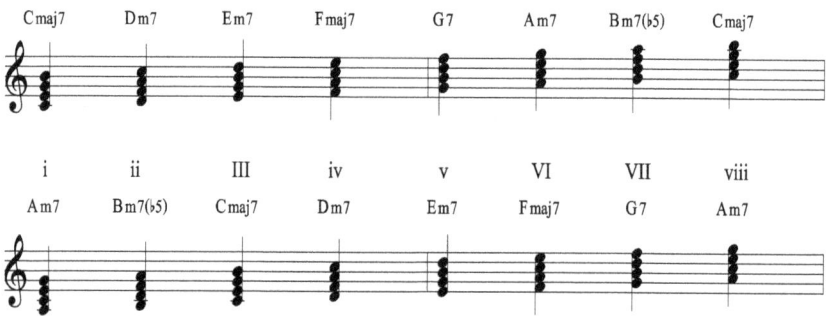

In addition to adding 7ths to the scale tone triads, you can keep adding extensions – 9, b9, #9, 11, #11, 13, b13, choices you would make depending on melody and context. When you see a chord called Cmaj7#11, do you know what to do? Everything that follows the C describes the quality of the chord and what has been added for additional definition and color:

1 We know the root of the chord is C, and we know it contains a major 3rd.

2 It's not just a C major triad. It also includes the first extension of the chord, the major 7th. Now the chord contains the notes C-E-G-B

3 The #11 is another color that further deepens the harmonic sound. If you count the degrees of the major scale, 1 through 8, and then keep going, you will get to the 11th degree, (F an octave above the 4th degree of the C major scale). When you add a #11 to the major 7th chord, you get a very dreamy, ethereal sound. The chord may also contain a major 9th, which is implied in the spelling.

If you don't already know this, it might be hard to make musical sense out of it until you go to the piano and hear what it sounds like. But this will acquaint you with chord spelling and notation that includes the chord extensions frequently found in jazz charts. They are very literal descriptions of the basic chord, its quality, and its extra bells and whistles. When you play these chords in the context of actual music, using appropriate chord voicings, you will appreciate how much they add to your harmonic vocabulary.

Functional Harmony

Movement as an element of melody and harmony have already been mentioned a few times, but let's look a little closer at the importance of this aspect of harmony. Functional harmony describes the way chords interact in tonal music. Some chords, especially in context, will indicate the tonal center, or key. As mentioned previously, tonal centers can be derived from the major scale or its relative minor (major and relative minor are just two of the many choices of tonal centers) Major keys tend to suggest brightness and minor keys ten to be darker. You may choose based on the lyrical content of your song. Some songs contain both, and the movement between a major key and its relative minor within one song is fairly common. Chord progressions often contain chords that move the music away from the tonic chord, and then move it back again as the music resolves.

The terms Tonic, Subdominant, and Dominant refer to chords based on the 1st, 4th, and 5th degrees of the scale. In the key of C, the music will often start with a C chord, a statement of the tonal center. After the C chord, there are many choices that will create harmonic development, moving away from the tonic, but eventually the music will return to C. The terms, "tension" and "release" are well illustrated by the relationship between the chord based on the 5th degree of the scale, the dominant, followed by the tonic. The chord based on the 4th degree of the scale, the subdominant, often precedes the chord based on the 5th degree, and these chords (in Roman numerals), I IV V (C F G in the key of C) are often enough movement to give the sense of beginning, middle, and end to a song. If we add another chord in the middle, the chord based on the 6th degree of the scale we'll have a **I vi IV V** progression that will ultimately resolve on the same tonic chord the song started with. Countless songs have been written with no more than these four chords, and sometimes even fewer. In jazz, the IV chord is often replaced with a ii (2) chord (D minor in the key of C), so the progression reads **I vi ii V.** In case you are unfamiliar with this common practice in harmonic musical notation, Roman numerals are assigned to the degrees of the tonic scale the chords are based on. Major chords are spelled with upper case letter and minor chords use lower case letters.

We've looked at I vi ii V progressions in relation to melody notes, but we're going to expand the possibilities of tonal harmony by adding some chords that can make a progression more interesting. Although there is plenty of momentum in the I vi ii V sequence, there are many more choices. I won't cover the scope of this topic completely here, but we'll look at a couple of samples that might open your ears. When you immerse yourself in music that moves fluently in the broader harmonic landscape, you may acquire a taste for these sounds that add layers of complexity and shades of mood. The following are two 8-bar sketches (one in the key of C major, and one in the key of A minor) that illustrate how you might add harmonic ideas to your scale tone chords. Notice that some of the chords don't occur at all in the C major scale or the A minor scale. Playing music in a specific tonal center does not restrict the use of chords that don't seem to belong there. If the melody notes are consonant with the chords, and they flow with rest of the melody, they can add unexpected, though musically satisfying, detail. Again, go to the piano and play these melodic/harmonic combinations. Which chords are based on tonic scale tones and appear in their unaltered form? Which have been modified in quality? Do they fit the melodies and seem to be part of the tonal center?

1

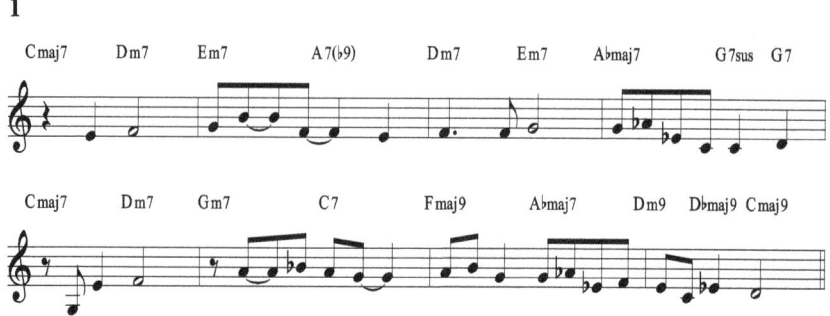

Secondary Dominants and Blues Chords

When you play scale tone 7th chords, the dominant chord that is diatonic to the key is the V chord. Using only the notes of the major scale, the V chord naturally contains a major 3rd and a b7. In the key of C, the V chord is G7 (G – B – D – F). This chord leans very strongly toward a resolution on the I chord, C major. But you can also play dominant chords on other degrees of the scale. Secondary dominants are commonly used to move the music forward and to give a different flavor to the music. A dominant chord contains a major 3rd and a b7th which implies movement toward a resolution and gives a brighter sound than a minor 7 chord. Be aware that when you use secondary dominants, dominant 7th chords with roots on scale tones other than the 5th, you will be adding accidentals to your chords and probably to your melodies too. Play the examples below and listen to the difference in sound and function.

Dominant 7th chords can also add a bluesy flavor to the music. When you play a standard 12 bar blues, most of the chords will be dominant 7ths, including the tonic. The most frequently used chords in a Blues are I – IV – V and they each contain a major 3rd and b7th. The dominant 7#9 chord which contains both a major and minor 3rd and has an edgy tension that lends itself to bending melody notes. When you combine these chords with Blues scale melodies, and a 12/8 rhythmic feel, the result is the simplest and most familiar sound of the *Blues*. The topic of Blues is much broader than this brief formulaic description, and like any other specific style of music, listening to the masters perform it is the best way to learn it. The power of the Blues is in its soulful performance. The inflections and subtleties of authentic blues must be heard to be understood and even then, the masters have secrets they may be reluctant to divulge.

Reharmonizing

Reharmonization is a fun approach to jazz arranging. Studying some examples of this, or doing your own, can also expand your harmonic concept in your compositions. Reharmonizing means altering the standard chord progression of an existing melody with substitution chords that are consonant with the melody notes but are not the original chords the composer wrote. Frequently a reharmonization is an expansion of functional harmony, but sometimes the new changes can seem randomly non-functional, held together by the thread of melody. Look at the examples below. Each 4-bar line contains the same melody, but different harmonic accompaniment. Notice the shift in the feeling of each set of chords, all heading toward the same destination, but arriving via different routes.

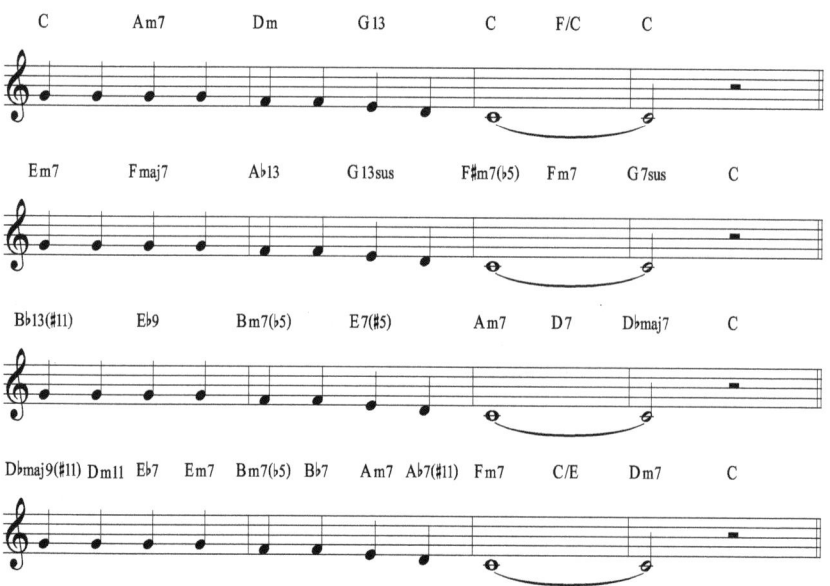

The examples above are just a few of the available choices. Context will influence your preferences but start thinking about being adventurous with the harmonic progressions in your own songs. The rules of harmony are flexible. Many contemporary recordings of jazz standards have been reharmonized in dazzling ways by highly skilled arrangers, and they give new dimension to familiar songs. Pianist/Composer/Arranger, Billy Childs, has done some gorgeously inventive arranging for singer, Dianne Reeves, reharmonizing well known tunes with great imagination and finesse. He manages to reinvent and enhance the source material without ever diminishing its original power and beauty.

Pedal Point and Slash Chords

Sometimes you will see chords spelled like this: A/G, Cm7/Bb, or Gmaj7/D. This is simply one chord played over a bass note that is not the root of the chord. In these examples, we're not just talking about chord inversions.

1. An A major chord with a G in the bass is a specific sound. The C# in an A major triad functions as a b5 or a #11 in a G major chord, and that sound could be spelled Gmaj9#11. We know the G chord has a major 3rd and that the 4th degree of the G major scale is raised a half step(#11). When you spell it A/G, it's very specific and easy to figure out.

2. Cm7/Bb is a Cm7 chord with the b7 in the bass. This most likely doesn't mean it's a Bb chord, but more likely a Cm chord that is moving. The Bb bass may be part of a descending bass line that is consonant with a Cm7 chord. You might find it among a sequence like this: Cm, Cm/B, Cm7/Bb, Cm6/A.

3. Gmaj7/D is a Gmaj7 chord with the 5th in the bass. This is not likely a D chord, but is instead a G chord, possibly in a situation where the D is a PEDAL POINT in which several chords in sequence are played over the D bass. When you see these chords in context, you will determine their function in relation to the surrounding chords and the melody.

These chords can get pretty far out, but like all chords, when you see them on a chart, you will look at the chords that surround them and what the melody is. Once you get the concept, you will begin to develop a vocabulary of chords spelled in this way and know right away what their function in context is. Just remember that the chord on the left side of the slash is played over the bass note on the right side of the slash. Play the example below so you can hear what these chords sound like.

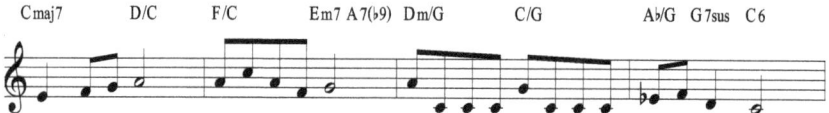

In the example below, the chords that are played over the Bb pedal point are not all considered tonally consonant with Bb, but the effect is a tension that releases with the last of the four measures.

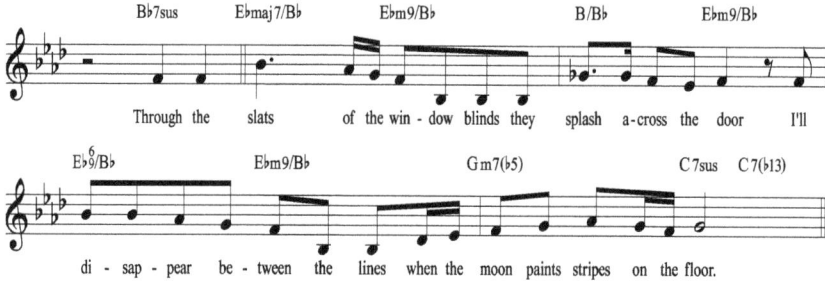

Sus Chords are chords that have a "suspended" scale tone, usually the 4th (occasionally the 2nd) that is not part of the fundamental chord. A dominant 7th chord with a suspended 4th will often resolve the suspended 4th down a half step to the third. This kind of movement can happen on any dominant chord and functions somewhat like an abbreviated ii – V. But the suspended 4th doesn't need to resolve and can function as a V chord, or secondary dominant in context. A dominant sus chord may also be spelled like a slash chord. Bb/C contains the same notes as C9sus (C – D – F – Bb) without a 3rd in the chord. Minor chords also often have a suspended 4th but will more often be spelled as a minor 11. An A minor chord with a D in it will likely be spelled Am11. Remember that the 11th degree of a major scale is an octave above the 4th degree of the scale, and you could call the chord Am7sus4.

To become fluent in recognizing and using these chords, check out some tunes in your jazz fakebook. Brazilian singer/composer, Ivan Lins, wrote a beautiful tune called "Velas Icadas" and it's full of dominant chords with suspended 4ths. You can hear how the additional note in the dominant chords creates movement when it resolves down a half step to the 3rd.

Non-Functional Slash Chords

Another way to use slash chords is in creating a spacious, atmospheric sound that doesn't necessarily imply a need to resolve to a destination chord. Using a series of these chords creates an openness and unpredictability of movement in the music. Each of the chords below could be spelled as dominant sus chords, but I prefer the slash chord notation. Notice that the roots of the chords are moving up in minor 3rd intervals. When the melody holds them together, they can feel like enormous clouds rolling by in the wind. The example below illustrates moving slash chords that are held together by the thread of the melody.

Chromatic/Non-Functional Harmony

This is where the sounds get really interesting. Non-functional harmony means that the chords do not function in a specific way to move the music toward a resolution. Even though they may be consonant with a single melody note because they contain that note, they don't necessarily have a "before" and "after" quality in moving the story forward. This approach requires a discerning ear. When you decide to try this option, you may stumble into *dysfunctional* harmony. Too many chords that are not grounded in function can make the music feel like it's suspended in nothingness. Again, melody and context are the glue here and a mix of functional and non-functional harmony, well placed within a strong melody can be gorgeous. Any note can be harmonized by chords rooted in every half step of the chromatic scale, and in some cases, several chords. Before this gets too confusing, look at this example and play the chords with the melody note. These are a sample but not a complete list of the possibilities.

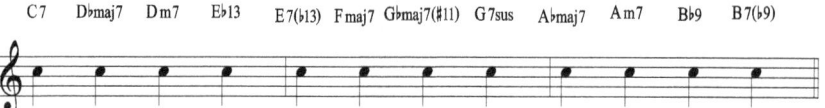

The following examples illustrate how non-functional chords can be used in the context of tonal music. The chords don't sound dissonant because of the corresponding melody notes. I've included two examples here of portions of my own compositions (as are all the examples used in this book) to show you how I like to add a little unexpected seasoning to my chord progressions.

1 EARLY SEPTEMBER (first 16 bars): This tune has an AABA form and the groove is a medium jazz waltz. It's in the key of Bb, but I took some liberties moving out of the key, choosing passing chords that are consonant with their corresponding melody notes. The resolution of the first 16-bar section is Gbmaj7, which seems to create a new tonic before it pivots back to Bb on the melody note – F, for the next section. The song does ultimately resolve in Bb after a bridge and final A section. For me, the melody is the glue here that allows for the harmonic wandering. I follow my ear and then make sure my choices sound cohesive.

2. **UNMERCIFUL (Chorus):** This song has a verse/chorus form, and a funky syncopated straight 8th groove. Although the central key is Dm, it modulates several times in the verse, and the ascending bass line through the first part of the chorus, adjusting the chord qualities to fit the melody notes. I also used common tones to create the pivot from

chords outside the key back to the tonic key. Melody is the glue and, in this case, the bass line grounds the cohesiveness.

Modulation

Another dynamic harmonic choice within the structure of a song is modulation, moving from the primary tonal center to a new key. It's somewhat common in pop music to repeat the final chorus of a tune a half or whole step higher than the key it started in. This dramatic arranging device is tried and true and elevates the intensity level of the music. It is also common to modulate between relative major and minor keys within the same tune. Many standards use this device, and a well known classic is "Autumn Leaves", written by Joseph Kosma in 1945, moves smoothly between relative major and minor throughout, starting in the major key and ending in the minor. When modulation is built into the composition, it can add layers of interest. Jerome Kern's Oscar winning tune, "The Way You Look Tonight" slides the bridge up a minor third before coming back home in the final stanza. Kern's masterpiece, "All the Things You Are" modulates frequently in the first three quarters of the tune, held together by strong melodic motifs. In the final stanza it pivots back to the original key on a single note that is consonant with the two seemingly unrelated keys. The result is high drama gracefully executed.

Common tones are effective in creating surprise modulations, but you can also set up a key change with a little harmonic intro, a couple of chords (like ii-V) that prepare the ear for the entrance of the new key in the next section of the tune. Modulations sometimes sneak in for a few mysterious moments and then move on. Mel Torme's "Christmas Song" is a tune I have to relearn every holiday season because of the trippy little shift at "folks dressed up like Eskimos, everybody knows…" I freely use modulation in my own songs, letting the melody lead me where it wants to go, and then adjusting the changes to fit. Sometimes I modulate so much that it's hard to pin down a single key signature. Master pianist/composer, Art Lande, gave me this advice: When you write out a tune that moves around frequently through different keys, just leave out the key signature and make your moves with accidentals. Problem solved.

The following 16-bar sketch illustrates how modulation can create melodic and harmonic interest in your writing.

But Do You Love It?

Ultimately, all this talk about theoretical concerns in writing is secondary to a more important consideration. Always let your ear be the boss. When you make moves that are interesting but not beautiful and satisfying, it's time to go back to the piano and work on it until you love it.

Individual chords and harmonic progressions don't have to be complex to be beautiful. Sometimes the truest and deepest thoughts and feelings are well served by harmonic simplicity. "The Water is Wide" is a traditional folk song, sometimes sung as a hymn. The chord progression and melody are simple, but profoundly beautiful. The emotional content of a song can be enhanced by the layers of sound color provided by sophisticated harmony, and there are songs with cowboy chords that are so gorgeous they make you cry. Remember: just because you can, doesn't mean you should. It's smart to increase your vocabulary and skill set and try new things, but are the chords you have chosen to accompany your words and melody expressing the heart of what you are writing about? I often end up trimming away the excess noise in my songs. Like Chopin said, (as played by Hugh Grant in the film "Impromptu") "Simplicity. It's the final thing".

While this book is not intended to give you a complete education in music theory, I've sifted through the important considerations regarding harmony in creative songwriting. Theory is a big subject. Those of you who are already fluent in this language can apply it to your own writing. Those of you who read this and feel like you need a translator, get thee to a theory class and learn this stuff.

Exercise 6: Adding Chords to a Melody

I have worked with songwriters who didn't play a chordal instrument. They sing me their melodies and I add chords to them. I usually go for the most obvious choices because I assume that's what the composer heard in their imagination. But there are many situations in which melody is simple and chords are sophisticated. For the melody below, add a chord progression that is obviously implied by the melody. Next, start over with a more complex chord progression, still consonant with the melody, but more nuanced and surprising than the first.

1   Note the key signature here. Are you in Ab major or F minor?

2   Key signature? Are you in F major or D minor?

Are you moving fully into the musical side of your song? If you have chosen a melody and some chords, have you explored what's possible beyond what you already knew? Have you tried a few chords that are more interesting than your usual handful? Is your song in a major or a minor key? Are you sure that your melody notes are consonant with your chords? At this point, many things may begin to shift and change. My high school art teacher, Jim Marta, gave me a valuable piece of advice: Don't be attached to your work. I hear that as encouragement to let go of things that aren't working, even if that particular melody, chord, or lyric seems exceptionally clever, poignant, or well crafted. If everything is pulling you in a different direction., go with the flow. You can always keep your unused ideas on file for the next song while you move on with the energy that is driving your current project. Sometimes we work a tune into chaos, trying so hard to implement every new idea we lose the heart of what we're expressing. If little tendrils of the tune are getting away from you, stop and ask yourself if you are still working on an idea that you love. Be willing to cut everything that interferes with expressing that idea. If you stay focused, you are ready to call what you have done so far a "first draft", and realize that there may be many before you feel your work is complete.

In the 1960s there was a popular song on the radio, sung by a woman with a very breathy, childlike voice. The words were kind of silly, and I hardly noticed the saxophone featured throughout. The song was "The Girl from Ipanema", the singer was Astrid Gilberto, and the saxophonist was Stan Getz. I was still immersed in the music that was coming to us from across the pond, the Beatles, Stones, Donovan, The Animals, The Hollies, The Kinks, etc., and when "Ipanema" came on the radio, I found it annoying. Little did I know then how much I would fall completely in love with Brazilian music in the 1970s and the writer of that song, Antonio Carlos Jobim.

We must give credit to American jazz musicians for bringing us the music of Brazil. Stan Getz collaborated with singer/guitarist Joao Gilberto and his wife, Astrid, and a trend was born. I have mentioned my fascination with Chick Corea and the stunning vocal music he wrote that featured Brazilian singer Flora Purim. And perhaps the most compelling of all for me is an album I have also already mentioned, "Native Dancer" by Wayne Shorter, that featured vocal performances by Brazilian composer/singer, Milton Nascimento. By the time I had moved to San Francisco from Seattle in 1976, I was hooked. I had no idea who Jobim was, but I listened to his recordings and loved them. There was a bass player who lived in the downstairs flat and one night he played guitar and sang the song, "Dindi" for me in Portuguese. It was a "died and gone to heaven" moment. I set out to learn what I could about this music.

In 1977 I was a barista in a little San Francisco cafe in the Inner Sunset called The Owl and Monkey. It was a local hub where poets, artists, politicos, and coffee addicts met and conversed by day, then live musicians performed at night. I was in my mid 20s and met some interesting people there, including a young man from Brazil who agreed to teach me how to sing some of Jobim's tunes in Portuguese. I was pretty good at faking the phonetic pronunciations of the words, and I could play the chords on my guitar. I didn't realize that many of the Jobim songs I was learning had been huge hits in Brazil. I would comp in the bossa nova style and sing these songs with sincere commitment to mimicry. Besides being very melodic, the harmonic sensibility of Jobim and his contemporaries was as rich as that of the American jazz standards I was singing. They eventually became an essential part of jazz repertoire, both vocally and instrumentally, and tunes like "Meditation", "Triste", "Corcovado", and "Paisagem" were often played by jazz bands. Later recordings by Jobim took a turn, incorporating the orchestrations of Claus Ogerman into his compositions. Jobim's quiet unadorned voice, surrounded by lush orchestral arrangements, was perfect textural contrast in these dreamlike tunes.

Brazilian music was evolving as musicians began to incorporate some of the influences of American pop music, expanding the samba grooves with funky hybrids. New artists were emerging, contrasting the gentle seduction of Jobim's music with more electric intensity. Toward the end of the 1980s, those of us in the USA who loved this music became acquainted with another Brazilian superstar composer by the name of Ivan Lins. He wrote gorgeous tunes, several of which had English lyrics (some by Marilyn and Alan Bergman), and they ranged in feel from energetic groove tunes to sensual romantic ballads. His harmonic approach was imaginative and deeply emotional, and the melodies were sublime. The songs soon found their way into the jazz fakebooks and we vocalists were performing titles like "The Island", "Velas Icadas", "Believe What I Say", "You Moved Me to This" and "Love Dance". The San Francisco Bay Area has a substantial Brazilian population, and he came often to perform sold out shows and concerts for his huge fan base. He would sometimes headline for a week at a time at a local club called Yoshi's, and I would go every night to listen to him passionately singing his tunes.

Brazilian music is beloved in this part of the world, and we even have a Brazil Camp that meets for several days every summer where students learn to play from local and visiting Brazilian musicians. If you want to further expand your harmonic and melodic world, check out some recordings by Caetano Veloso, Guinga, Hermeto Pascual, Egberto Gismonti, Djavan, and Milton Nascimento. All are brilliant composers and musicians. There are also many American musicians who have recorded these tunes, and many American composers (including me) who emulate these guys in their own writing.

Tips

1. Make sure you own a few good fakebooks. "The Standards Real Book", by Chuck Sher is a nice collection of tunes, and the changes are jazz versions, meaning they are accurate as played in a jazz setting. Many standards have gone through a "correction" process after years of being played by musicians who have a love of optimal harmonic content. There are several good fakebooks out there, but books that have "jazz" in the title seem to be of higher quality.

2. Harmonic analysis is a good exercise for getting inside the changes of a tune. You look at the melody, and the chords, and then analyze the movement in the progression, from a mathematical and theoretical point of view. This is a very instructive practice. How does this chord work with that chord? What key is this part in and what key is it modulating to? How is the modulation actualized – with a ii-V set up for the new key, or a pivotal common tone? What are the intervals and scale tones in the melody? What exactly is going on here? What do you notice that you have heard in other tunes?

3. Transpose, your own tunes or other songs you know. Transposing your songs into different keys helps you to sync up the numbered scale degrees and functions of melodies and harmonies with the actual letter names of the notes. Many of my students resist doing this, but any fluency I have in theory came to me from doing countless handwritten transpositions of standards for myself and my vocal students.

4. Notation software is a wonderful thing. I have been using Finale for years and, especially after writing hundreds of charts by hand over the years, it's a miracle. It requires learning the program, but it's intuitive and the manual is easy to understand. The editing capabilities are phenomenal after years of white-out and cutting and pasting charts. And of course, once you enter a piece of music and store it in your file, it's there when you want it, and you can edit it easily if you need to.

5. Piano is the best instrument for learning theory. The physical layout of the keyboard makes visual sense in the way that a guitar neck doesn't. You don't have to be a pianist to use the piano keyboard as a tool for understanding the structures of chords and scales. Even someone who has never played a piano can quickly learn the names of the keys, and the nature of whole steps and half steps.

6
RHYTHM

A well played groove in any tempo or time signature is a source of energy, attraction, and deep satisfaction in music. It's also an element that requires attention and precision in solo and ensemble playing. We think of the drums as the centerpiece of the time, but all the instruments, including the voice, are engaged in creating a groove that's full of life. When the time is off, it's uncomfortable, and when it locks in and feels relaxed, it makes everybody play better. Songwriters who don't play drums, or play with drummers, can certainly have strong rhythmic sensibilities and still create plenty of energy with simple guitar or piano accompaniment even if there are no drums in the mix. Rhythm has a cerebral side, but the fun part is how it feels in your body. Writing a song, we get to decide what the rhythmic feel will be, and that decision is worthy of consideration.

Groove Driven Music

Rhythm can be a primary driving force in a song. We are attracted to music because of the way it feels, and a great groove is a magnet for elevating your mood. We are always in pursuit of meaningful lyrics and intentionally crafted melody and harmony, but sometimes these elements take a back seat to the powerful way rhythm can get you moving and just make you feel better. If the rest of the song is truly terrible, the groove might not be able to save it, but if the song is reasonably good, the groove can make it great. A simple melody and changes, with lyrics that are little more than superficial fluff, can be enough if the real reason you love the song is that the rhythm gets under your skin and makes you move. A few years ago, the song that we all heard several times a day was "Happy", by Pharrell Williams. It's a well crafted tune in many ways, with a light hearted lyric. Every version I heard seemed to capture the good natured, life affirming pleasure of the message and I never got tired of it. "Rollin' in the Deep", by Adele, has a dark earthy pulse that holds back nothing. I love it even though I can't recall the words and the melody is very repetitive. There are countless examples in jazz of groove driven music, vocal and instrumental. In fact, one of the measurements of a successful jazz track or performance is the question, "Does it swing?" (Hoping for a resounding "Yes".) If you write a song that revolves around its rhythmic components, write the rest of the music with the groove in mind and let it be the star of the show.

Time Signature

TA: *A time signature is one of the first things you will write on your manuscript paper (or select in your notation program). If you don't know the time values of notes and rests, please seek out this information. Understanding what beats are is fundamental. A 4/4 time signature is called "common time" for a reason. A very high percentage of western popular music, like swing, rock, ballads, country, and folk to name a few, are written in 4/4, i.e., 4 beats per measure with a quarter note (or rest) representing one beat. Other choices could be 3/4 waltz time, 12/8 might be a slower blues tune, and 2/4 could be samba. It's fun and challenging to play with "odd times" – asymmetrical signatures like 5/4 or 7/8.*

A groove that drives the whole tune with shifts in dynamics, but not tempo or time signature, is the standard approach, but occasionally you may want to change these elements within a tune. It may be that just one phrase seems to need a couple of extra beats, so in a 4/4 time signature, you may add a bar of 6/4 or combine a bar of 4/4 with a bar of 2/4. These "extra" beats may provide breathing space or emphasis that feels necessary, and you can rely on your ear to tell you if it makes sense musically. Time signatures can accommodate little quirks and left turns without undermining the flow. The rules of musical notation are flexible and meant to serve your inspiration rather than confine it. We are used to tunes having a regular number of bars, usually a multiple of 4, but if asymmetry serves the music, go for it. You also have the option of writing whole sections of a song in different time signatures (and tempos), and a shift like this can indicate a change of mood, or a contrasting part of the story. The structures of rhythm can be fluid, but since time is one of the unifying elements in music, be sure to flag in rehearsal any eccentric choices your band is not expecting. I encourage exploring these kinds of rhythmic moves but only when they feel natural.

Here is an example of a 4/4 time signature with a bar of 2/4:

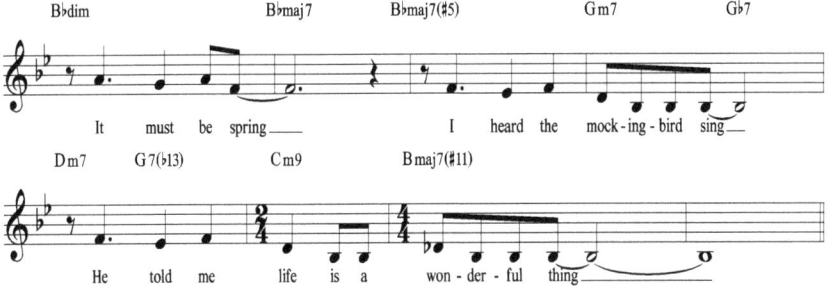

Quarter Note Subdivisions

One of the defining aspects of a rhythmic style is the subdivision of the quarter notes, combined with rests and accent beats in distinctive patterns. Are you playing in straight 8ths (downbeats and upbeats of equal duration), or swing 8ths (with a triplet subdivision – longer downbeat, shorter upbeat)? How about a 16th note subdivision like funk, or a folk fingerpicking style? Sometimes a groove can be hard to pin down with a concise label, especially if it is a hybrid, a groove that combines elements of different styles. The broader your experience with many styles of music, the easier it will be to give it a rhythmic description. Ultimately, what you call it is less important than the way you play it, but it's interesting to listen closely to different grooves and observe what beats, accents, and other details make them what they are. When you write a chart, putting a brief general description of the groove written in the upper left corner will be helpful to anyone who is reading it, and it may still require more verbal explanation or demonstration on an instrument. The following list contains some samples. There are many styles not mentioned here, but you will get the idea, especially if you have a clear understanding of the fundamental structures of time, beats, rests, accents, etc. The components of any genre can't really be reduced to rhythm only, but it's an important factor, and will inform the choices in your own songs.

Straight 8th Grooves

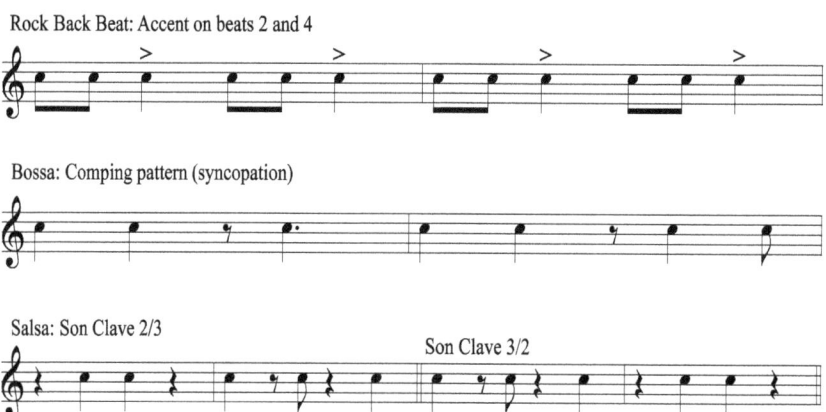

A straight 8th groove derived from music that was released on the Northern European record label, ECM, is common in jazz. It flows, often through partially arpeggiated chords, with no set accent patterns, though it can groove like mad. Some of the well-known artists who have recorded on the label are jazz musicians, Keith Jarrett, John Abercrombie, Art Lande, and Charlie Haden. While the rhythmic feel referred to here is by no means the only aspect of the music created by these master composer/musicians, it is a distinctive component of the ECM sound. The clear and spacious precision of the music has a modern classical flavor with a jazz sensibility. The writing evokes a prism of moods, with adventurous melody and harmony rendered with emotional and cerebral depth. This rhythmic approach has now achieved the status of a style label that composers sometimes use to describe the rhythmic character of their music: *Straight 8th ECM*.

Triplet Based Grooves

A triplet-based 8th note, also called a *Swing 8th*, is what characterizes a *Swing* groove. You will hear this in any style of swing music, from Big Band tunes from the 1940s, like Duke Elllington's "Satin Doll", to a contemporary jazz swing feel, which may have an edgier intensity. One of the sounds you will likely hear in a swing tune is a "walking bass line", quarter notes played on the bass with strong swing lilt, both grounding and creating momentum in the music. A *Shuffle* groove is a Rock version of Swing, combining a rock back beat with a Swing 8th, like in the song, "Kansas City". We usually think of Swing as a 4/4 time signature, but a *Jazz Waltz* also has a Swing 8th, and you can hear the difference when you compare a Jazz Waltz to a traditional waltz, although both have a 3/4 time signature. "Better Than Anything", written by Bob Dorough, is a well-known Jazz Waltz.

This is what a *Swing* triplet-based 8th note subdivision looks like in 4/4. The first 2 beats of the 8th note triplet are tied so it sounds like a longer downbeat and shorter upbeat.

Blues tends to be a triplet-based groove and will either have a 12/8 time signature or a 4/4 time signature with an indicated 12/8 feel. Writing out a melody in 12/8 is somewhat more complicated than writing it in 4/4 and indicating that it has a 12/8 blues feel. There are many ballads that adapt well to a blues interpretation just by changing the straight 8th to a 12/8 feel.

The pop music of Jamaica, *Reggae*, is often played with a triplet-based groove. The emphasis in the guitar comping pattern is usually on the up beats – 2 and 4. Listen to Bob Marley's "Is This Love" for a great example of this style. Marley, a singer/songwriter, was considered one of the pioneers of reggae and was probably the most well-known reggae artist in the music world.

Gospel, another style that originated in African American culture, is often played with a triplet-based feel. The piano is prominent in this music, which originated in the Black church, but influenced popular music too. Superstar, Aretha Franklin, began her singing life in the church, and in 1972 she recorded a live performance with a choir in the New Temple Missionary Baptist Church in Los Angeles called "Amazing Grace". It sold over 2 million copies and won a Grammy for Best Soul Gospel Performance.

16th Note Subdivision

In contemporary popular music, especially African American styles, *Funk* is the music that features a 16th note subdivision. When the quarter note is divided into 16ths in this style, the result is a uniquely energetic but cool groove. Even when the 16ths are implied rather than articulated in every measure, the rhythm invites dancing. This is a groove that happens in layers of syncopation, with very active comping, and a bass part that accents prominent beats in the bar. Think of Chaka Khan's recording of "Ain't Nobody" or Grover Washington Jr.'s "Just the Two of Us". The vocal parts are rhythmically driven, but the music also creates a foundation for soaring sustained-tone vocals. Ballads played in a funk style may have a more spacious vocal with a subtle but rhythmically active groove. Remember "Baby, Come to Me" by James Ingram and Patti Austin? Downright seductive. *Funk Shuffle* is related to funk with its 16th note subdivision but has an internal swing in the way the 16ths are played. Think of Al Jarreau's "We're In This Love Together". This is such a fun and catchy groove and is a kind of rhythmic hybrid.

It seems that nothing could be further from a funk groove than *Folk* and *Country* music, but finger picking on the guitar or banjo are commonly 16th note patterns. It makes sense when you think of the way the hands fit the strings on a guitar. "Gentle on My Mind", a song by Glen Campbell, is a beautiful example of finger picking. It's very hard to replicate this feel on the piano. It seems to require the lightness of strings and the close proximity of the fingers on the strings to achieve this precisely delicate accompaniment, and of course it can be played at any tempo.

Samba is also a 16th note based rhythm, but the time signature is 2/4, with a bass accent on beat 2. Bossa Nova is more frequently written in 4/4 with a straight 8th subdivision, so why the 2/4 in Samba? I've heard Bossa described as "United Statesian" in its interpretation of time, and Samba accentuates the more authentic sensual side-to-side movement of Afro-Brazilian dance. Samba tends toward bright tempos, though slower samba grooves are mesmerizing. When those of us in the northern climes delve into the intricacies of South American rhythms the subtleties are sometimes lost, but we appreciate the infectious joy of Samba and the celebratory ensembles that play in the street during Carnaval. Brazilian master teachers of this style visit the States, and jazz musicians are often drawn to the melodic and harmonic content of the music along with the rhythm.

Hybrid Grooves and Layering

You aren't confined to one groove or the other in creating your own music. Once you have an idea of the vibe of your song, you will decide an approximate tempo, and perhaps a "ballpark" idea of the rhythmic style you want. If it fits neatly into a category with a label, that can simplify things when you are playing with other musicians. Once you have chosen a time signature and decided whether you want a straight 8th feel, swing feel, or 16th note subdivision, you can begin constructing the musical components that will give your song a stylistic foundation. But sometimes a groove is ambiguous and not easily labeled. Don't let that stop your rhythmic explorations even if you have to make up a name to identify the style of your song. Play with different tempos before settling on how fast or slow your song should be.

Songwriters generally have some facility on a chordal instrument. Piano and guitar are the common choices, and they function a little differently from each other. The piano has a big range of options, capable of providing melody, chords, bass, and comping patterns, and you don't have to be a virtuoso to play around with these functions when you arrange your song. Guitar can supply rhythmic comping, strumming, fingerpicking, and single note melody or bass.

I write at the piano and my songs have a more pianistic flavor, though I love having a guitarist on a gig or a session. I can play bass parts on the piano, but a real bass player on electric or acoustic bass knows better than I do how to get the job done. In performance, I work with actual living instrumentalists, but in arranging my songs, I try for at least a skeletal idea of what the layers of sound will be in creating my groove. And I always prefer working with a drummer who has a lyrical sensibility, rather than just holding down the time with patterns. It's fun to start with a tempo and general idea of the feel, and then build it from the ground up, assigning beats and functions to different instruments, or trusting them to improvise. When you create an interesting comping pattern and add a bass part, where might you add other instruments to fill out the arrangement? Background vocals? Horns? Strings? Mandolin? Bells and whistles? When you listen to studio recordings of intentionally arranged music, you will likely hear that care has been taken to add parts that complement, rather than imitate or cancel each other rhythmically. When the voices of each instrument have been assembled with care, is the result cohesive? Is there a "greater than the sum of its parts" interaction that makes the groove feel alive and connected? You don't just want a bunch of disparate parts that are zigging and zagging in different directions. In a catchy groove all the parts coalesce into a unified sound that has a center and moves like an animal, all the arms and legs in graceful motion, heading for a destination.

Tempo

Tempos are a big factor in making a tune work, and I tend to be meticulous about them. Too fast or too slow can wreck an otherwise well written tune. It's worthwhile to see where your song lies naturally. In jazz, for instance, ballads are often played more slowly than they are in other styles. The space between beats may seem very wide, but this can also be an opportunity to phrase creatively. Too slow, and it's hard to maintain the energy, even if your phrasing is brilliant and other instrumentalists are filling in the gaps. On the other hand, if the tune is too fast, it may be hard to keep the feel relaxed, not to mention getting all the words in. But a bright uptempo tune that is below the "freak out" threshold can be exhilarating, even if it challenges your chops (practice slowly and then increase the tempo). Pop music tends to be in the middle with tempos. Ballads, which are often accompanied by chords played on the quarter note, are rarely dramatically slow, and "uptempo" does not usually mean burning fast. A steady stream of medium tempos can be monotonous. In the wedding band days, there were segments in the celebration where we played for several unbroken minutes to accompany the immediate family dancing with the bride, with the groom, and with each other. We would seamlessly segue from one medium tempo Bossa Nova to the next, which we referred to as "Bossa Nova Hell". We loved the tunes but did not love the monotony of the medium tempos.

Whatever the tempo, the important thing is the visceral feel of the time. It should support the music and move it along. If you suspect your music is rhythmically fuzzy, practice with a metronome. You want to feel it in your center, allowing it to engage you without effort. Most of us left to our own devices tend to drift, rushing or dragging the time, and a metronome can be very grounding. Using prerecorded drum patterns to practice with will keep your tempos honest, and will supply more detail to interact with, inspiring more creative rhythmic phrasing. You, me, and everyone else in a musical ensemble must learn to feel time internally while listening for the *collective time feel*. You know it when you hear it because it's so seductive it calls you to it.

Syncopation

If your strong melodic syllables lie only on downbeats, they can feel boxy and wooden. Using dotted notes, tied notes, emphasizing upbeats, phrasing across the bar lines, and placing rests strategically, make for a kind of rhythmic counterpoint within a steady groove. Some styles of music have syncopation built into them. Swing, bebop, samba, and salsa, for example, really move when the whole band is creating the syncopated groove together, each one taking a part. You might hear syncopation naturally but have a hard time reading it or writing it out. I practice it by sitting at the piano and setting the metronome to a slow tempo. Then I keep time in 8th notes, moving my palm up and down on a surface like the top of the piano with my left hand, while playing a syncopated melody with my right. My music of choice for this exercise is the Charlie Parker *Omnibook*, a collection of rhythmically complex be-bop tunes and transcribed solos. If you care to start with something simpler, try some tunes by Antonio Carlos Jobim. It always helps me to learn something using multi-sensory input – tactile, visual, and aural. Eventually it gets easier writing things out that have complex time figures.

If you are not fluent in reading and writing time, practice playing syncopated rhythms like the illustration below. Jazz and Latin music are full of syncopation and learning to read and write time that dances around the beat will expand the rhythmic phrasing in your own writing. Set the metronome to a slow tempo to practice complex rhythms, then gradually increase the tempo. A grid of 8th notes below the measures can also help you visualize the phrases. Remember, using eyes and hands in addition to ears increases facility in learning.

Rubato

Playing or singing freely without any specific meter can be expressively dramatic, and there is an art to it. The music may be written with a time signature, but you are not adhering to a set tempo. You can perform a whole song this way, but the tricky part is to keep it moving. There is a tendency on the part of many pianists to fill each pause in the vocal line with grand flourishes of arpeggiated chords. For me, this is overkill and interferes with the delicacy of this kind of phrasing. I prefer the phrases to flow like speech, some faster, some slower, a few pauses, a moment or two of suspended drama, but keeping a pace that doesn't get lugubrious. A common way to use rubato effectively is to contrast it with time. The standards we often sing in jazz have what is called a "verse", an intro-like section at the beginning of the tune with melody, lyrics, and changes (not to be confused with verse/chorus form in contemporary songs). Singing the 8 or 12 measures of verse without tempo, in a conversational manner, makes the entrance of the groove an event in the music. If you are working with other musicians, you will need to work out how the time comes in. I like to sing rubato verses with a single chord instrument, hold a fermata on the last note, and have the pianist or guitarist set up the time with a few pick-up beats. When the rest of the band joins the music at the start of the refrain, it should sound tight and intentional, rather than stumbling into the music. You want to create a clean contrast as the energy shifts. You can insert rubato sections into the body of your song but think through the way you want the rhythmic transitions to occur. Even if it's a little more complicated to change tempos and key signatures, or throw in a few moments of rubato phrasing, doesn't mean you shouldn't do it. Just understand that in order to pull it off you need to plan logistically.

Percussion

Many singers who don't accompany themselves on piano or guitar are skilled with percussion instruments, a shaker, tambourine, guiro, etc. Playing these instruments while singing requires a strong time feel and a steady hand. If you aren't working with a full drum set, a little percussion can give plenty of rhythmic grounding to the music if it's done well. I have done many trio gigs with a percussionist instead of a drummer and I love it. The lightness and clarity of a cajon, for instance, can drive the groove without overwhelming the music. I choose the drummers I work with carefully and when they set up with an array of percussion instruments in addition to the drum set, that's an additional bonus for me. I don't like to compete with the volume of the drums and appreciate when the drummer is really listening and participating, rather than just locking into a pattern and barreling along oblivious to the dynamic detail of the music. I'm especially sensitive to this when we're playing my original songs.

Singing the Groove

The voice is a rhythm instrument if you sing with rhythmic awareness. The way you articulate your words and melody in relation to the time can either enhance the groove or dilute it. Words have great percussive properties. Clearly articulated consonants and well-defined syllables can really make a groove light up. You may want to place your notes precisely on syncopated beats or place them on beats that are not articulated in the pattern of your groove. You can also play with a contrasting vocal approach, floating your melody over an active rhythmic accompaniment. When you're feeling the time in your body, playing around with rhythmic placement can be more interesting than bouncing along on beats that are already being played by someone else in the band. Throwing in some triplets over a 4/4 time signature, or singing straight 8ths over a swing feel, add interest to the time. You can begin a phrase on any beat in the measure, and using rests to create space allows a melody to breathe. Be aware of what the rest of the ensemble is doing when you're singing a rhythmic tune and lean into the group time feel. Even counting in a tempo can convey groove if you have internalized it. The idea is to participate in lighting up the rhythm, so it feels effortless, natural, and fun.

Exercise 7: Playing with Rhythm

Choose a standard tune, something simple to begin with, like "Autumn Leaves", "Pennies from Heaven", or something more contemporary that you know well. Now play and/or sing it in a few different rhythmic styles. Jazz vocalists do this all the time in performance. It's fun to sing a ballad as a medium swing tune, or a double time feel bossa. Change the time signature from 4/4 to 3/4 or 5/8. For example: I once wrote an arrangement of Johnny Cash's song "I Walk the Line" as a bright samba with Brazilian style changes. After you try a few different grooves with a standard or two, experiment with your original tunes. Your songs might work in a variety of styles, and then you have the fun of choosing which groove you like best.

Are you still working on the song you started with? How are you addressing the rhythm? If you are accompanying yourself on piano or guitar, does your instrumental part include the groove? Will you be playing your music alone or with a band? Drum set or percussion? If you are working with computer multi track recording programs, record your song with a drum pattern and add a bass part. This will inspire you to sing more rhythmically. Even a ballad can hold together more effectively with simple rhythmic accompaniment. Working with drummers and bass players is big fun, and the first time I rehearse an original tune with an ensemble comprised of actual human beings, I find out whether or not I hit my musical target.

If you are curious about rhythmically interesting music, ask the rhythm section. I have worked with numerous drummers and bass players who turned me on to music I would never have come across by accident. And since the focus of this chapter is rhythm, what better place to visit than the mighty cultures of Africa that have given so much to our musical landscape? Please check out the artists listed here. Their music is available online. It will be an addition to your musical awareness and vocabulary, and it's a joy to listen to. Notice the complex layers of rhythm and the exotic vocal phrasing. Some traditional instruments of West Africa are the djembe – a hand carved drum, balafon – like a vibraphone, kora – a stringed instrument, and gourd shakers. Ensembles may also include electric guitars and bass, and other instruments found in contemporary western music.

In the late 1970s a singer, songwriter, and multi-instrumentalist from Nigeria by the name of King Sunny Ade *became one of the first African pop musicians to receive international acclaim. His sound was labeled "juju" music, with songs derived from the Yoruba tradition. The music has a strong rock flavor, and features electric guitars, talking drum, synthesizers, vibraphone, and clarinet. The ensembles were large, including dancers. Multiple layers of sound created an exciting environment for the vocal melodies and harmony. In 1982 he received a Grammy nomination for his album "Synchro System", a first for a Nigerian artist. He toured Europe and North America to critical acclaim and once recorded with Stevie Wonder.*

A few decades later, music from Mali made its way to the West. Wassoulou music was dominated by women musicians, and notable among them is Oumou Sangare, *known as the "Songbird of Wassoulou". She composes her own songs and writes about the status of women, in marriage, and in the culture at large. Since the 1990s she has performed in prestigious venues around the world, including the Melbourne Opera, and the Oslo World Music Festival. Her music is rhythmic with layers of traditional instruments supporting the stunningly beautiful vocal sound of multiple singers. The melodies are complex, accompanied by repeated instrumental patterns, with traditional instruments. The vocals have an improvised quality interspersed with tightly arranged sections of unison singing. Oumou Sangare was a featured singer on the "Imagine" recording by Herbie Hancock, along with Pink, Seal, and India Arie.*

Cameroon has given us some wonderful musicians, among them Etienne M'Bappe, *a bass player, singer, and songwriter. He is a masterful instrumentalist with a warm, rich vocal sound and sings in his native Cameroonian language. His harmonically captivating music is a hybrid blend of African, funk, rock, jazz, and classical, featuring lyrical melodies and layers of instrumentation and additional vocalists. He has played with numerous western musicians, and tours with guitarist John McLaughlin. Another Cameroonian bassist who has a high profile among jazz musicians in the west is* Richard Bona. *He is also a singer, guitarist, and percussionist. He travelled to Europe for his education, and now lives in New York and has recorded with numerous American musicians, including the Brecker brothers, Joe Zawinul, Branford Marsalis, Chaka Khan, and Bobby McFerrin.*

Nguyen Le *is a Vietnamese musician who lives in Paris. The range of his music is very broad, and I'm including him among the artists of Africa because of an album he recorded with several North African and Arabic musicians, called "Maghreb and Friends". The album was recommended to me by both a Latin jazz drummer and a fusion jazz electric bass player, and when I heard it, it became one of my favorite recordings of all time. The originality, and superb musicianship is staggering, and I don't use the term lightly. The complexity of the writing and playing, not to mention the diversity of moods, grooves, and instrumentation is pure joy. I had it playing on repeat in my car so that every time I started up the engine, there it was, knocking me out repeatedly and keeping me driving in the groove. Nguyen Le is a master composer and guitarist and his recordings are all quite different from each other. He has released compositions based on Vietnamese folk music, and another album is a tribute to Jimi Hendrix. But this one demonstrates a particular alchemy of influences that is rare. As disparate as all the tracks are, it holds together, like a great book or movie with different chapters and scenes, all telling a single story. If you listen to one album I have mentioned in this book – make it this one.*

Tips

1. Playing or singing complex rhythms well hinges on chops – muscular coordination. Just like anything you do with your muscles, including your vocal folds, informed reps are everything. Start slowly and gradually increase the tempo without losing your precision. The goal is to internalize the time so you can relax and play/sing with ease.

2. Practice playing percussion instruments. Use a metronome and start slow. Keep playing until your patterns are relaxed and accurate, then speed up the tempo little by little. Play along with recordings.

3. Drumming circles are popular and often open to non-professionals. I lived across the street from the Bart station in Berkeley, CA for 12 years and all day every Saturday and Sunday as many as 20 or 30 drummers would be playing together from noon until 10pm. At first it drove me mad, tempting me to drummercide, but when I got used to it, I grew to love it.

4. A fun time-related detail in composing and arranging is the addition of instrumental rhythmic hits, or short figures of rhythmic/melodic instrumental notes that occur between sections, or at other points in the song. This is common in jazz arranging or in styles of music that use horn sections, like R&B.

7
FORM

Songs come in containers, and those containers hold the ideas, feelings, and musical dynamics being expressed. A song form is like a house with different rooms, and usually has defined sections that are separate, but also part of the whole house, the whole song. There are traditional forms and forms that are more open in their approach. And like a house, you may move through a song and find graceful symmetry and balance, and you may find surprising little closets under the stairs. What we're usually going for is a strong relationship among all the parts of the song, even parts that may contrast in ways that seem a little eccentric. Regardless of the cupola in the attic, the glass walls of the sunroom, and the secret science lab in the basement, the song should sit on a good foundation that holds it all together. It's one song that starts on the first note and ends on the last. I suggested earlier that you make your song about ONE THING, one central idea, that lives under one roof, at one address. This is not a limitation, but instead is a way to focus and give a clear identity to what you are creating. Form is one of the elements that give clarity to your ideas. If you have more ideas than your song can hold, write more songs.

How Does Form Work?

But enough of the poetry. What does form mean? I've already mentioned that repetition is a way to bring cohesiveness to a song. If you write a song without sections of repeated material, and just keep adding ideas, it won't be long before it loses any sense of structure. That might be okay occasionally but can sound confusing and musically weak if we are meandering with no defined purpose. It might be hard to even think of a song that doesn't contain thematic repetition of some kind. Let's look at how we might approach the different sections of a song and how we refer to them.

I have been listening to pop music all my life but have not studied the forms with the intention of writing songs in that style. However, these forms are so ubiquitous, they seem to organize the sections of music by default because of their familiarity. I'm sure there are variations, but the most common form in contemporary pop songs is: Intro, Verse, Pre-Chorus, Chorus, Repeat, Bridge or Instrumental Break, Pre-Chorus, Chorus, Outro. These sections usually, but not always, appear in symmetrical numbers. Pop songwriters tend to underscore these fixed elements. The sections that lead to the chorus introduce the story and describe in some detail what the chorus will ultimately reveal. The pre-chorus bumps the energy level up a few notches, sometimes with a harmonic shift. These sections are designed to lyrically and musically set up the moment when the chorus arrives, opens up the energy, and delivers. An effective chorus is simple, repetitive, and catchy, and usually contains the title of the song. It often moves to a higher vocal range than the verse and pre-chorus and is the dynamic high point of the song, the "ear candy", the *hook*, the payoff, the punchline, the fun phrase that everyone remembers and sings along to. This is one template. We will be looking at other options for creating form in ways both traditional and flexible, while keeping intact the idea of the container for the song's one core idea.

Components of Form in Songs

1. An **INTRO** is usually an instrumental set up to the beginning of the song and the entrance of the voice. Its function is to introduce the rhythmic groove, key, and tempo. It's usually short, often 8 bars or less. Intros can also be more inventive, longer, and not necessarily musically derived from the main body of the song. But however imaginative an intro is, it should deliver the vocalist to a graceful entrance.

2. The **VERSE** in contemporary popular music is the beginning of the story, the "once upon a time" part of the song that introduces the subject

you are writing about. Musically, it is often low to moderate in intensity, so there is somewhere to go when the drama begins to build. This is where many of the details of the story are revealed, and they may complement or contrast what is coming later. Often there are a couple of verses in the beginning of the song before a new section is introduced. In folk music, the form will often be a verse followed by a chorus, and that order is repeated, telling the story in the verse, and repeating the chorus after each chapter. Leonard Cohen's song, "Hallelujah" is an example of folk style verse/chorus form. **Stanza** is another word that refers to the verse.

3. In standards from the Tin Pan Alley period of songwriting, the **VERSE** is a section of the song that precedes the refrain. It only occurs once, and in the days of musical movies and plays, the verse set up the transition from spoken word to song. These sections were short, usually fewer than 16 bars and did not necessarily contain material drawn from the refrain, though the lyrics were introductory to the theme of the song. In performance, this type of verse is often sung in a rubato style. When the rhythm enters with the refrain, it creates an effective dynamic moment of contrast, and can serve as a satisfying "event" in the presentation of the song.

4. The **PRE-CHORUS** is a contemporary term and occurs mainly in pop music. It is placed between the verse and the chorus to create dramatic energy and rev up the emotional content, as if to say, "This happened, and you won't believe what happened next….". Its function is to increase the tension that will be released when the chorus arrives. It may be similar musically to the verse but should be different enough to function as it's meant to. The melodic range may shift to higher notes, and the intensity of the chords and instrumentation also increases, signaling that something big is about to happen.

5. The **CHORUS** in pop and folk music is what the song is about, the destination of everything that precedes it. Here the music gets bigger, ascends in pitch and volume, and usually shows some contrast to the verse and pre-chorus. It is the highpoint of the song, often lyrically condensed and musically simplified. It's written to be repeated and contains maximum emotional intensity. This is where the tension releases into the satisfying resolution to all questions, in bold unmistakable strokes.

This is also where the lyrical content is abbreviated and direct in relation to the storytelling that precedes it. Some songwriting methods suggest that you write the chorus first, since it will function as the centerpiece of the song. An effective chorus is magnetic, may contain the title of the song, and is the moment of maximum intensity.

6. The **CHORUS** in the standards of Tin Pan Alley, is also called the **REFRAIN**. This is the part of the song that is most familiar, and in fact, many of the verses that were written for these songs have long been forgotten. The refrain is the melody we recognize. Within the refrain are further divisions in sections. Standards are generally (not always) 32 bars long and the 32 bars were divided in sections of 8 bars: The first two sections of 8 bars were similar, followed by an 8 bar bridge, which took a little musical detour before returning to the final 8 bars which were similar to the first two 8 bar sections. This form is referred to as AABA. A common variation in this template is the ABAC form in which the first and third 8 bars are similar, and the second and fourth sections of 8 bars are different. In jazz, a **Chorus** refers to the recognizable composed melody of the tune, regardless of length or form, played or sung after the intro and the verse (in songs with a verse). An improvisor will play over the harmonic material of the chorus after the melody has been stated. A performance may feature multiple improvisors, each playing one or more choruses before the song ends with another chorus by the singer or instrumentalist reprising the melody.

7. Not all songs contain a **BRIDGE**, but this is an interesting section that aims to contrast musically with the rest of the material and add more detail to the story. This is a good place to modulate if you are so inclined and it should stand out musically in some way that is distinctive and obviously different from the other sections. This is a good place to bring in contrast that complements the lyrical theme. The bridge usually has a destination and may precede an instrumental break or a final chorus in a pop tune. In a 32 bar standard, the bridge is the middle section of 8 bars. The ending of the bridge can be a dynamic highpoint that leads to the final stanza before the end of the song. This section functions in the same way regardless of the style of the music.

8. In pop music, the **BREAK** is an instrumental section that adds breathing space to the story. If we've already had a couple of verse,

pre-chorus, chorus sections, and a bridge, we're getting ready for the home stretch. The break may or may not follow the harmonic progression of some section of the song. In jazz, the instrumental **SOLO** functions specifically to allow the various members of the band to improvise before the final vocal sections of the song, and extends and develops the composed material of the song. In jazz, the improvised choruses are often as important, if not more so, than the composed material of the chorus.

9. A **CODA** is an additional section that may simply extend the final chorus or create an ending to the song. It might be a **VAMP** section, or perhaps a more elaborate version of the ending, with additional bars. Sometimes a vamp becomes another part of the song that escalates in energy before a fade ending. Or a coda might be a simple sentence or two that wraps up the story. The term **OUTRO** is the opposite of Intro and is simply a defined ending, with or without vocals.

Form in Action

1. Taylor Swift is one of the most prolific and successful singer/songwriters in contemporary pop music. She has a strong voice, decent guitar chops, and is a good lyricist. Her songs tend to follow the pop template in form. I recently listened to her song **LOVE STORY**, and here is the map of the form. Listen to the song and follow along.

    Instrumental intro: 8 bars
    Verse 1 – 8 bars
    Verse 2 – 8 bars
    Pre-Chorus – 8 bars
    Chorus – 8 bars
    Verse – 8 bars
    Pre-Chorus – 8 bars
    Chorus x2 – 16 bars
    Instrumental interlude – 8 bars
    Bridge – 8 bars
    Chorus – 8 bars
    Chorus modulates up – 8 bars
    Outro: repeat and fade chorus chord progression with vocal accents

2. Now let's look at the form of a well-known standard written by George and Ira Gershwin, **SOMEONE TO WATCH OVER ME**. Again, the terminology of verse and chorus are used differently in this style, but the bridge has a similar function. In a jazz setting, the instrumental solo would occur after a full vocal chorus, over the changes of the first two A sections, with the vocal re-entering at the bridge. A full performance would likely be the verse and two full choruses (with an instrumental interlude after the first chorus). Also, let's assume this song is being performed as a ballad, even though standards can be interpreted in different rhythmic styles.

Intro: Sung in a rubato style, the intro might be a simple ii-V set-up
Verse – 24 bars (this one is exceptionally long)
A – 8 bars
A – bars
B – Bridge) – 8 bars
A – bars
AA – Improvised instrumental solo
B – Vocal comes in at the bridge
A – Final vocal section
Ending: Could be a simple ritardando, or a tag.

Beyond Tradition

The examples above are typical to their styles, but there are often exceptions. I tend to let my song show me its form. I listen for what should happen next. I'm not tethered to traditional song forms, but certainly use variations of them often. Sometimes a song will slide easily into a common form, with a balance of verse, chorus, and bridge material. I also love the approach to form used by Laura Nyro, one of my first influences in songwriting. She was very adept at changing keys, tempos, and moods within her songs giving them a cinematic feel. The glue that held them together was the story she was telling, the emotional content, and her vocal sound. There was nothing contrived about all the shifts and transitions in her music and the authenticity of her inspiration was actualized in high level artistry.

Several years ago, I was writing songs for a musical theater piece. The tunes I wrote for the project were longer than usual and structured in non-traditional forms. Once I gave myself permission to follow my imagination, the songs seemed to naturally evolve beyond the tried and true with enough connecting thread to keep them cohesive. I encourage inventiveness in this aspect of writing but would underscore the necessity of knowing what you're writing about, so you don't lose your core idea in a form that's too complex. Let's go back to the analogy of song sections being rooms in a house. If you think of your music as the furniture in the rooms, you can place the furniture, the notes and rests, anywhere in the room, but not outside of the room. Form matters. Let your ear be your guide, and don't be afraid to try something and then discard it if it isn't working. There is always another option. No matter how far out you dare to get, cohesiveness is important.

Song forms, traditional or otherwise, allow you to develop your one main idea while showing different aspects of it. Try some adventurous things to delineate the different rooms in your house, the sections of your song. You can do it with harmonic and melodic transitions, and you can change time signatures, tempos, and keys. You may discover some imaginative ways of problem solving in making sure the different sections connect with ease. This is a detail of craft that requires attention and care. As mentioned earlier in the Harmony chapter, setting up a modulation with a brief harmonic intro, even one or two beats, prior to the entrance of a new key can make this shift easy on the ears and natural sounding. Melodic common tones that pivot between keys are a dramatic way to move into the next musical room. Rhythmic shifts can be a little more complicated, especially changing tempos. You can conduct these transitions in performance, but a good chart and some rehearsal will help you to pull it off. Figuring out how to make your ideas work logically and gracefully is part of the fun. If you want to be daring in your explorations of form, just realize that performance with other musicians will probably require extra time and preparation. But if you do the work, the results could be exciting and lift your music to higher levels of interest.

Song Length

How long should your song be? In my early songwriting life, my songs were fairly short, 2-3 minutes max. I did not think in terms of arranging them to extend the length through more repetitions, additional material, or instrumental sections. The ideal length of a pop tune has always been about about 3 minutes. We assume the listening audience has an attention span that wanders after that length of time and begins seeking new stimulation. In jazz, the "head" of a song (the fundamental written material that identifies the tune) may be somewhat brief, setting the stage for improvised solos. But a 32 bar standard for instance, will include solos sandwiched in between the "in" chorus and "out" chorus extending the length by several minutes. When I write my songs, I often include sections for instrumental improvisation, sometimes over the form of the song, but because my song forms may be somewhat complex and irregular, I often write sections specifically for instrumental solos. These will be harmonically related to the body of the tune, contrasting or complementary, but more compact and symmetrical than the body of the tune. I like instrumental interludes and feel they add dimension to the story. Sometimes my students don't write enough music to make the song feel complete and their tunes are over before any development occurs. You might suspect that you haven't quite completed your thought in a satisfying way when it feels like something more is supposed to happen. You will probably realize when it's too long or too repetitious, and has become monotonous. I tend to think of the right balance as an intuitive decision, but it may take some time and writing experience before you can make a good judgment call on the perfect length of your song.

It's nearly impossible to be objective about your own songwriting when you are first starting out. You will want to get feedback from someone who has more experience. But ultimately you want to be able to step back from your work and listen for the balance and cohesiveness in your song form. If it feels lopsided or incomplete, it probably is. Sometimes we get so far inside the lines and spaces of the process we need to put the whole thing down for a day or two, and then come back to it with fresh ears. I have at times been in such a hurry to finish a tune that I wasn't honest with myself about how satisfied I was with my work. But then it nags at me until I address the weak links. I never fully stop until I love all of it. I want the container and everything I've placed in it to measure up to my own musical integrity and sense of beauty and balance.

Exercise 8: Analysing Form

Listen to the songs on the following list. Write down the form analysis of each one. How would you define the sections in each song? Do they follow a common template? How are transitions achieved – harmonic pick-ups?, melodic shifts?, modulations? changes in the instrumental arrangement? contrast in the lyrical material? is there a dynamic energy arc? how does the song begin and end? do the sections balance and complement each other? is there an obvious hook? Does the song unfold and keep your interest, or is it static? is there enough repetition? Does the whole thing feel cohesive, like different rooms in the same house?

1. Ain't Nobody – Don Wolinski (recorded by Chaka Kahn)
2. Happy – Pharrell Williams
3. Lush Life – Billy Strayhorn
4. New York Tendaberry – Laura Nyro
5. God's Plan – Drake

How is your song coming along? Have you finished it yet? Are you on to the next project? Ask yourself if you have written honestly about ONE THING. Even if it's one thing with many details, does it have a central thread that defines it? Have you created a reasonable balance between new material and repetition? Does the length feel right? Have you shortchanged anything? Did you push your imagination to move past common cliches and into a true statement about the feelings you are representing? If you had to add something, what would it be? Have you played it for anyone? Do you love it? Have you received any feedback? Are you glad you're a songwriter? I'm very glad you are a songwriter.

The Beatles arrived in my musical world when I was 12. Their music was perfect for a pre-teen girl who was sick of piano lessons with the nuns. The body of work they left us evolved dramatically over the span of a few years between 1963 and 1969 when they were writing and recording. Their early, catchy, pop ear candy was a delight, but the music began to get more interesting as the culture of the 1960s progressed. Each successive album was more adventurous than the one that preceded it, and their creative originality was dazzling on every level as they began to really own their unique compositional and lyrical voices. They managed to captivate mainstream audiences while letting their imaginations run free. The songs were inventive, whimsical, deep, cryptic, impressionistic, socially relevant, and in some cases, stunningly beautiful and moving. They inspired other musicians who heard what they were doing in the studio with orchestration and recording techniques, and within a few years, their influence was unmistakable. What a wonderful time to be young and in love with music.

Two albums from the middle years of their musical reign were "Rubber Soul" (1965) and "Revolver" (1966). Both presented a range of lyrical themes and musical moods unlike what other groups were doing. "Norwegian Wood" was (and still is) confusing and humorous and was the first pop tune that featured sitar. "Michelle", and "In My Life" have a classic, well-crafted feel and have been covered countless times. "Here, There, and Everywhere", "For No One", and "Eleanor Rigby" are lyrically captivating, emotionally moving, and musically mature, especially when you realize these were guys in their 20s. There were lighter songs too, with humorous lyrics and heavy rock grooves, like "Taxman", "Drive My Car", and "Good Day Sunshine". More than a half century later, these songs are still circulating, and holding up as substantial compositions. There are several jazz interpretations of the Beatles' music, and the songs lend themselves to reinvention.

In 1967 the Beatles released "Sgt Pepper's Lonely Hearts Club Band". This album was heavy on the whimsy with songs like "When I'm Sixty-Four" and "Lovely Rita", but there were more serious themes too. "She's Leaving Home" is a bittersweet portrait of a girl leaving her parents' world to break free into a life of her own choosing. Perhaps the stand-out dramatic piece is the one that closes the album "A Day in the Life". The detached, somewhat sardonic tone of the narrative delivers critical commentary on modern life and depicts the apathy of watching the days go by and being spun out by the unrelenting pace of it all. When I was a teenager, the world was going through a cultural paradigm shift and this music seemed to arise from that energy and make perfect sense. Looking back, it seemed to us that we were living in a relatively innocent time, but we had all graduated from the earnest post war values of the 1950s. The world around us was changing fast, with major political figures being assassinated, the Vietnam War, and throughout the culture, life was shifting. The Beatles said so much without literally saying it, and we were eager to hear it.

"A Day in the Life" was also the first song the Beatles recorded that really expanded the concept of form in pop music. It starts in a moderately slow 4/4 tempo in the key of G and proceeds for a couple of verses, in a somewhat understated manner, with a tale about reading the news and seeing a film. There are a few touches of absurdity in the lyrics and this section ends with a reference to getting high (at a time when this was still considered pretty edgy). It slides into a transition that begins with a series of ascending chords and morphs into a continuous upward slide that delivers the song to a new key and rhythmic feel. This section is in the key of E and while the pulse stays the same, the groove changes to a double time feel. The music and lyrics have a frenetic energy and give an impression of someone anxiously hurrying through his meaningless life. Toward the end of this section another reference is made to getting high and a transition of harmonic movement leads to a reprise of the first section in the key of G, keeping the double time feel in the rhythm. There is another stanza much like the ones that opened the song, followed by a cacophonous orchestral ascension at the end that is punctuated by a momentary brief pause, then a single loud E major chord. Nothing like this had been done before in pop music and fans like me were surprised and thrilled at this exciting and unexpected turn that would prove to be an example of how form would evolve in the years to come.

The Beatles went on to record several songs on their last couple of albums that used the idea of form loosely. On "The White Album", the song "Happiness is a Warm Gun" is short but has four distinct sections that are very different lyrically and musically. It moves from beginning to end with no repeated material, shifting quickly from one idea to the next, but somehow it all fits in a vaguely impressionistic manner. We had become accustomed at this point to lyrics that were either too hip to understand, or clever sounding with no obvious meaning. On their final group album, "Abbey Road", a song called "You Never Give Me Your Money" has five distinct sections. All are different lyrically and very loosely connected musically, but the song seems complete. It starts in a wistful mood in the key of Am, picks up tempo and moves to Cmaj, and after a guitar section that rapidly modulates, the song finally ends with two sections in Amaj. You have to wonder if they were getting a little reckless by this time, patching things together because they could, and knowing their fans would love it because it was so hard to define. Our parents were locked out.

This expanded approach to songwriting began to infiltrate popular music and artists who were recording in those years were inspired to broaden the concept of form, a trend that continues. When I listened to the Beatles, I just loved what they were doing and didn't analyze it. I knew they were onto something I would one day understand. In my teenaged heart, it was good because it was the Beatles. They were a phenomenon that vigorously rattled popular culture at just the right time in my life. Way back then, I had no idea that my life's path would be that of a professional musician and music teacher. But after I heard the Beatles, I got my first guitar. More than half a century later, music still has me under its spell.

Tips

1. Common practice in writing out your tunes, either in full notation form, or lead sheet, includes labeling the sections. Sections of the form are usually labeled with the letters of the alphabet. The rules for this are not absolute, and the point is that someone reading the chart would know where they are in the music, in rehearsal and performance.

2. In musical notation there are signs that work like a road map if you are moving forward and then going back and repeating part of the song. Using repeat signs with first and second (or third) endings allow you to repeat material without having to write it out again. Coda systems are also a way to navigate back to a repeated section, and then possibly jump forward to another section.

3. Using too many repeat signs and coda systems can present a problem for musicians reading the chart. You may be correct in your use of these navigational tools, but the chart may still be confusing to read. My preference in some cases, with a complicated form, is to write out the sections in order without repeats. It makes the chart longer, but it's worth it if it means the music will be played correctly, especially if the finished chart is under 5 pages long, so that it fits on a music stand and doesn't require turning pages while playing. It's not fun to look over at the pianist during a concert and see that face of panic with the thought bubble above his head, "Oh no!! Where are we??!". Remember that playing someone's original songs requires an impeccably accurate map.

4. If you have a specifically composed intro or ending, write them out. A good intro can borrow themes from the tune to set up the key and tempo. A composed ending is good punctuation at the end of your story, unless it feels appropriate to create a vamp/fade ending, as in a recording.

8
PRESENTATION

Do you have a finished song? This next step on the songwriting path is where it really gets fun. When you have composed music and lyrics with care and said what you meant to say in a cohesive and balanced form, and you love it all, it's time to think about getting the music played and performed. It is always a thrill for me the first time I rehearse new material with a band. If I have put my attention to writing a clearly readable chart and given any additional detailed verbal instruction to the musicians, this will be the moment I know if my ideas are working, if something in the composition needs to be revised, or if the chart needs to be written out more coherently.

Do You Love It?

This is the most important question to ask yourself when you feel that you've completed a song. The answer is very subjective, but this is not a question to ask someone else until you've answered it for yourself. Often, when students are seeking instruction in songwriting, they will try so hard to follow the rules and suggestions of the teacher or the method book, that they forget the original inspiration of the song in the effort to get it right. It's common to rely on the opinions of your instructors when you are first starting out, and it's satisfying and encouraging to receive affirmative comments about your work. But the internal buzz, the electric visceral energy, the spark of feeling that lights you up, your *love* for what you have created ultimately belongs to you. Yes, framing your inspiration in good songcraft is important, but remember the opening chapter of this book that underscores the most overwhelmingly important element in a song: The way it makes you feel. Is the whole greater than the sum of its parts? Did the alchemy of all the components result in something beautiful that touches your heart, makes you want to move, makes you smile, makes you cry? You will learn to recognize when you have gotten there in your songwriting journey, because when you find it, nothing anyone says about your song can dim the light of your honest artistic experience. It may take time to get this, but don't listen to your song through other people's ears.

Everything you write is a steppingstone that leads you to your best work, your most honest expression of your truest feelings. Sometimes the songs that move you the most are full of flaws and loose ends. Please tend to them with care, and use your skill set to aim high and correct the choices that aren't working. But don't fix what isn't broken as you attempt to follow the rules. I tell my students that my suggestions for improving their songs are my point of view, but the real authority is their own experience of their original music. They are free to reject my suggestions and when they do, I get out of the way. I have received comments from musicians I consider masters regarding details of my songs, and I always listen and consider their comments. But I only change something if I agree my work will be improved or enhanced by their opinions. It took a long time for me to own the right to validate my choices, my own taste, and what feels right in my original music. You'll know when you no longer need someone else to give you their seal of approval. I hope that by the time you are reading this, you have created a song you love, a song about one true thing that holds up on every level. Now what?

Musical Notation

A beginner piano book will teach you the letter names of the lines and spaces in the bass and treble clefs, time values of notes and rests, and how these symbols translate to playing the music on keys of the piano. I highly recommend studying good fake books and reading through tunes you are familiar with to see how the notation looks. Transposing songs you know into multiple keys is a good way to become fluent. Rhythmic notation, especially syncopation, is often the most challenging part of reading music, and it's a good idea to start with simple music, playing with a metronome. I often nudge my students to learn musical notation if they don't already know it, and sadly, many are not motivated to do it. I consider it a measure of serious musicianship and a valuable skill to master in documenting your original songs and communicating with other musicians. Call me old fashioned. I think it's important to be able to read and write the language if you don't want to feel like a tourist in the world of music.

Charts

When you purchase sheet music for a song you want to sing and play, you receive a substantial amount of musical information, i.e., guitar tabs, chord symbols, the melody written on the top staff of the stave system, with lyrics written below their corresponding notes. Below the melody staff there will be an additional two staves with a two-handed piano accompaniment, usually a reduction of a larger arrangement. This is great for some accompanists who are not used to improvising, but who may have well-honed sight-reading skills. In some circumstances this may be the way you choose to write out your original music, but often it's more information than is really required to get your music played.

Lead sheets are an abbreviated way of writing out music that contains enough, but not too much information. Many pop musicians and nearly all jazz improvisors not only know what to do with a chord symbol, but also bring their own musicality to the situation. A lead sheet contains the fundamental key and time signatures, perhaps a metronome marking for tempo, the melody of the song written out in full, chord symbols written above the bars, and lyrics underneath their corresponding notes. You can write additional directions at various points in the music to further explain the rhythmic feel and mood of the song, and at transition points to clarify what happens next. Because time signatures can be interpreted in so many ways, it's good to write a brief verbal description of your groove in the upper left corner of the chart, i.e., *medium jazz waltz, bluesy ballad 12/8 feel, straight 8th ECM*, etc. In rehearsal you may have to further explain the feel of the music and if there are any eccentric moves in your songs, alert the musicians both on the chart and verbally. Writing out your tunes in lead sheet form is a good way to document them and is often sufficient for rehearsal and performance. I know that some songwriters create beautiful music but lack the skills to write out their songs. If you are serious about writing music, learning to do this is a worthy investment of your time, and an efficient way to share your music with other musicians.

PRESENTATION

THEORY ALERT: *Check out the lead sheet for "The Chart Song" and the map of signs and symbols that follow. Charts in this form can contain a lot of music, and they will always contain melody, chords, and lyrics, with the song form clearly apparent. I try to limit charts to 4-5 pages so they fit easily on a music stand and instrumentalists don't have to turn pages while playing. Sometimes I will opt for writing things out in full rather than using repeat signs and coda systems – again for easy reading. The most important thing about a chart is getting the music read accurately in rehearsal and performance, with enough information, but not too much.*

Reading the Map (See Example above)

1. *The title of the song, the composer(s), a brief description of the rhythmic feel.*
2. *Time and key signatures*
3. *Intro: An improvised instrumental intro only needs the chord symbols above the bars. You can also write a melody into your intro if you want something that specific.*
4. *This song is an AABA form and the letters are written in caps to note the sections. In current common practice it is more likely to group the first two 8-bar sections and label them A, followed by the B section (bridge), and the final stanza is labeled C.*
5. *The music of the first 8 bars repeats and this is written with a first and second ending. When you get to the end of the first 8 bars, you will choose the bracket with the number 1 in it, and the repeat sign tells you to go back to the top and sing the second line of lyrics. At the end of the second 8 bars, you will take the second ending, the bracket with the number 2 in the upper corner, which takes you to the bridge.*
6. *This bridge is 8 bars long and is indicated with the letter B.*
7. *After the bridge, you will sing the final 8 bars. You will then see a Coda system with the directions to go to the sign (at letter B.) and play through to the coda, which is at the end of the first 4 bars of letter C. When you get to the first coda sign, you jump ahead to the next coda sign, which is the last line of the music and the ending of the song.*

Many other things can happen in a chart, but this is a pretty standard example of how it's done. Sometimes you have to do a little fancy adjusting and arranging of the material so that it gets played the way you want to hear it. Music notation can accommodate most of what want to happen, and you can also add text in a chart that further explains directions. Sometimes, there is no avoiding having to verbally describe what you mean. It's worth it to hear the music you envisioned being played the way you heard it in your head.

Notation Software

As a songwriter who does lots of editing, I find notation software extremely valuable. I used to take great care making beautiful handwritten charts using a felt tipped calligraphy pen, but with this method is you must rewrite them if you want to edit anything. And as much as I love the look of handwritten manuscript, computer generated charts are more clear and easier to read. If you have spent years writing things out by hand, the editing capabilities of programs like Sibelius and Finale are miraculous. These programs cost a little but are well worth it. There are also free notation programs available online. Changing keys, adding bars, fixing mistakes, moving around whole sections of music, can all be done quickly and easily once you get a handle on the program. The user's manual in the Finale program is very clear and specific and you can probably teach yourself the dozen or so moves you need to make a lead sheet (If I could do it, you can). Most programs also have an option for playing your song into the program via a connected piano keyboard, and it will create notation. Just be aware that it transcribes accurately, so if your time is off, it will write exactly what you played, even if it's incorrect. I discovered that I often play behind the beat when I saw my playing transcribed accurately – it was a mess. When you enter your songs into the program all your music is conveniently stored in your computer for printing and editing. Committing your music to professional looking notation is a statement that you take your work seriously and the musicians reading your charts will do likewise when they don't have to struggle to read them.

Demo Recording

Recording your songs in a program like Garage Band or Logic Pro is an excellent way to stand back and hear your original composition, and to offer it to others as a demo. Connecting a keyboard and microphone to your computer is simple. The programs have built in sounds that convert what you play on the keyboard to a wide array of different instruments. You can play with rhythm loops, change tempo and key, move sections around, overdub your lead vocal, and add vocal harmonies. Once you learn how to use these tools your music is much easier to share with others, and a great reference resource if you are planning to record the music in a professional studio.

I often start the demo recording process by choosing a rhythm loop. Even something light, like a shaker, or congas, will function as a metronome and add a rhythmic flavor. The next layer will usually be the piano part. My digital keyboard can become a Steinway grand in the computer. A bass part would be the next addition. Of course, a real bass player in a real recording studio would be ideal, but for demo purposes, the piano can play the part and the computer can turn it into an acoustic or electric bass. With my computerized trio tracks in place, I will most likely plug in a microphone (usually with an interface box) and add a lead vocal. When I'm satisfied with the vocal, I may then start adding some other fun sounds. I love vocal harmonies, so that may be the next step. Maybe I want a cello or a French horn in the mix, or possibly an electric guitar solo, or an acoustic guitar comping sound. Whatever you decide, this process is big fun, and gives you something to play for other people. It's important to do your best in this demo recording process. You don't want to play your songs for other people and have to explain ahead of time that it's just a demo and it doesn't sound as good as a real studio recording. Most listeners will not bother to try and imagine the better version.

Many people are doing their professional recording at home with high end recording software. Files can be passed around to other instrumentalists and singers to add layers of arrangement, and then on to a pro engineer for mixing and mastering. This process can also be filmed and used for promotional videos.

The Impact of Good Singing

Let's face it. Great singing elevates any song we write. A mediocre song that is performed by a wonderful singer has a fighting chance of making an impact, even transcending the mediocrity of the material. A wonderful song delivered by a mediocre voice may not make the impact the song deserves. An excellent song performed by an exceptional singer is a stellar combination, a thing of beauty that sails out into the air to reach the ears of those waiting to hear it. Will you be the one performing your original songs? If so, do you need some voice work before you're ready to give your song the vocal it deserves? Take some lessons or do some practicing on your own to get your voice in shape. If you are writing for another singer, do you have someone in mind? Think about the vocal quality that best expresses your words and music.

There are trends in popular vocal music, and once they have taken hold in the ears of the general public, everyone tries to sound like them. Currently it seems to be very popular to sound young and breathless, whether male or female, with a childlike affectation and understated detachment. Another sound is the bright, intense, voice, which usually at some point in the music becomes a passionate, louder, higher, heart-on-your-sleeve belting sound, clearly stating joy or angst in no uncertain terms. R&B vocals are often very impressive, featuring voices that are strong and smooth, with full ranges. One of the identifying features of this style is the addition of ornamental melismas, which seem to be almost a requirement, though to my ears, less is more. Some styles of singing seem more athletic than musical to me, but that's an aspect of singing and instrumental playing that many people enjoy. Imitating trends in vocal styles may interfere with the development of a personal sound. Most vocal styles have a certain amount of affectation that obscures naturalness, whether it's a contrived blues sound, jazz, theater, country, or any number of other styles. You may choose a singer for your song based on your preferred style, but make sure they really get your music and can interpret it well. The vocal performance is the delivery system of your original song so make sure it enhances your writing without overwhelming it.

Arranging

What to add, what not to add? Arranging is a big subject with many facets. There are people who specialize in this area of musical creation, working with bands, orchestras, choral groups, and individual artists to fully actualize the many dimensions of the music. Like choosing (or being) the perfect vocalist for your song, how you arrange your material can have an impact on how it is received by an audience. You may be able to arrange your material yourself, but if you lack this skill set, find someone to write your arrangements. Many musicians have experience doing this work and it's worth the expense of hiring them if it means that your songs will be heard with the dynamic qualities that bring them to life. Strings, horn sections, and specialty instruments can add dimension to your writing and underscore the emotional content, but if your imagination is cinematic and you want a great big sound, that may involve many more musicians, and greater expense. It's big fun playing with these toys, but never rely on extra sounds to fix something that needs rewriting. Make sure your song holds up in a simple guitar or piano/voice rendition before dabbling in additional sound color. Think carefully about adding musical elements that would be difficult to reproduce in a live performance.

Studio Recording

When you are ready to record a professional quality album, you will probably want to work with an engineer in a recording studio. Instead of a computer generated bass part played on a keyboard, you will hire a real bass player who plays an actual bass in real time. There will be actual drums with a bunch of high quality, specifically placed microphones surrounding the set. A real high end grand piano will often sound better than a digital one, often because it's more fun to play, and that will also require a pro set up of mics. You can record your music live, with everyone playing together, as in a concert performance, but this requires a precisely detailed set up and does not allow for the ease of editing you will have with a layered approach to recording. If you are confident that you and your musicians are rehearsed and ready, a live recording can capture the spontaneous energy of a show, which sometimes gets lost with multitrack studio recording. But if you decide to go the overdubbing route, you can record basic tracks and a scratch vocal first. The final vocals and additional instruments can be added later, and you will be able to edit each track individually.

If you don't know how to navigate this process, hire a producer. The producer's job is to pull together all the elements that bring the recording to life. They will listen to your music and help you decide how big the production will be, how many musicians will be involved and the sequence of each track of the arrangement. Rehearsals and recording sessions will need to be scheduled. Rehearsal space will require the gear necessary for all the musicians to do what they do (most pro musicians have their own gear). You will need to pick out a recording studio, and a producer should have knowledge of what's available, including the cost of studio time. If the producer is a skilled musician, he or she will give input on how everything is going during the sessions, helping you decide if the recorded tracks are as good as they can be and if the music is taking shape the way you envision it. I have always produced my own work and have produced the projects of other singers and songwriters. But I think it's a good idea, if you don't have comprehensive knowledge of how to get the job done, to hire a producer you trust. Be sure to discuss your budget ahead of time. I have seen projects explode in cost when a producer has free reign with a project the artist is paying for.

Mixing and mastering a multi-track studio recording involves more time and expense and you will want to work with an engineer who knows how to get the best sound out of recorded tracks. A good mix, enhancing and balancing the sound levels, can make your music outstanding, while a bad mix can wreck it. I love the experience of recording an album in the studio. Every part of the process, from making the charts for the tunes, to the final mastering of the music, the design and graphics, and the release concerts, are fully engaging and satisfying. This effort to present original work in its best light is well worth the time and expense. Music is an ephemeral thing. Capturing it in a high quality recording allows it to live on, to fly out into the world, and to make connections with other musicians and audiences.

Video: The Industry Standard for Sharing Your Work

Alas, these days CDs seem to be more or less over, and streaming platforms are also a flooded marketplace that gives little return on investment. But there is another way to spend your cash getting your music into the eyes and ears of the world and make an impact. Whether you use your phone to record a video of yourself in your music room or hire a producer to create something more dazzling and elaborate, people want to see you performing your music. Now you not only have to sound great, you also have to look great, and it might even be fun moving into this medium. The first place I look when someone mentions a musician I might like is Youtube. In spite of the flaws inherent in many online platforms, there is a reason why people flock to them. Many people no longer own expensive sound systems and instead listen to their music via their computers and phones. In an everchanging cyber world Youtube may not be forever, but the medium of music videos is here to stay. Videos are practically a necessity for a successful personal music website.

The DIY approach can be functional if you are deliberate in setting up your sound and lighting and using adequate recording equipment. Even if you are just recording on your phone, you will want to have decent mics and speakers if you are playing live in the room. Even at the low end of production, choose a visual setting that has a desirable ambience. At the very least, if you are going to sit on the edge of the bed, make sure the bed is made and you are wearing a clean T shirt.

A performance video of a live gig is beneficial documentation of your music if the quality is good. A bad performance committed to video is probably not something you want to post on Youtube or on your website. You can find nearly everything you need to know about this process online, so don't get scared if you don't have a clue how to make it happen. A professional videographer will do this work for a fee and help you create something you can feel proud of. Many of the videos that are presented these days, even by the talented amateur crowd, are of reasonably high quality.

You can also create videos in your computer that feature music you have already recorded. Putting together a series of photos, or little snippets of action that illustrate your music is much simpler than producing an actual movie of your song. This approach may not be super impressive, but it's very accessible to anyone with a computer. It might be considered a path-of-least-resistance approach, but it still could make more of an impact than an audio recording on Soundcloud or Bandcamp. Large scale music video productions that have a script and many scenes are another level of commitment that will cost more money and take more time. An experienced producer knows how to make this happen start to finish, from creating a story, mapping out the action, perhaps including actors, costumes, make-up, a variety of indoor and outdoor sets, and all the post-production work.

Performing Your Songs

Do you plan to perform your music live? If you are interested in showcasing your original material in performance, you will want a good recording that is available for listening by booking agents and club owners. There are several public platforms online, like Soundcloud, Bandcamp, and Reverb Nation, that allow you to make your music accessible for listening, and Youtube is the platform for videos. Having your own website that features samples of your music, in both audio and video versions, along with information you would like to share with your listeners is an option. A website or EPK (electronic press kit) is an essential promotional tool that can be easily accessed by whomever is booking performance venues.

What kinds of rooms are most conducive to the performance experience you are seeking? In bars and restaurants, the music may not be the primary reason people are there, and you may have to contend with all the noise and distraction of eating, drinking, and talking. You may be dreaming of stadium shows or large concert venues. Pursuing this level of visibility will take time, energy, and money, but why not reach for the stars? My personal preference is small concert venues and house concerts. I like the intimacy of these settings and want my audiences to come because they choose to listen to an hour or two of original music. I spent many years singing in noisy commercial venues, but rarely performed my original music in these rooms. I take enormous care to write and arrange my songs and I want to present them in settings where they are the main event.

Nothing has been more thrilling to me musically than playing my songs in a concert setting with a band of highly skilled musicians. I love what the instrumentalists bring to the table. I love the rehearsals that happen ahead of a gig, where we work out the bugs in the music and clarify the details that make it sparkle. Preparation is key to a successful gig and it's your responsibility to tend to every aspect of the process. The reward is the peak experience of releasing your creation into the world and casting a spell over your appreciative audience.

Sales: The Big Hustle

It's a challenge to make money in the music business in the 21st Century. Artists who are at the top of the heap, getting lots of exposure, touring, selling merch, etc., are still able to garner wealth, but this is a very small percentage of the music that is being created. There are many streaming platforms now that sell music in digital form and most people now listen without physical objects like records or CDs. In fact, the whole recording industry has been in trouble for years due to the availability of streaming platforms that pay the artists almost nothing for music that costs thousands of dollars to create. But let's save that discussion for another day. What really matters, and I mean this from the heart, is that you are a creative person who is doing your best to write and perform music that didn't exist before you made it.

If it is your intention to get your songs placed in movie, a TV show, or a commercial, this book is not the best resource in that regard. If you want your songs to be recorded by other artists, there is no foolproof method for making this happen. If you are trying to get your songs to the artist you are interested in, sometimes their label, production company, or management can be the conduit. This will be another chapter in your songwriting journey, but not in this book. My comments are not meant to discourage aiming high in setting your goals, and if you have the talent, work ethic, and commitment, why not? Songwriters who dream big are the ones who are placed in films and television, and with artists who are looking for great original material to perform and record.

If you have read through to this point, you know that writing music from a personal artistic sensibility is not the same thing as creating commercial product. This has always been the lament of artists – high quality original music may not be everyone's cup of tea if it doesn't imitate what's popular. Mainstream audiences often want to listen to music that sounds familiar and is easily relegated to the sonic wallpaper of their lives. But artists create because they must, regardless of the outcome. So don't be discouraged if you have loved every bit of the process of creating your music but it's not paying the bills and has also been a little costly. Other people spend their money on ski trips, fancy restaurants, sprawling homes, and great shoes. Art is something that you own because it lives within your soul, and nobody can take it away from you.

Exercise 9: Perform Your Song

Play your song for someone else. If you are already a performing musician, play your song on a gig. If you perform at open mics, play your song. If you attend songwriting salons, perform your song. Play it in as many circumstances as you can get away with. Don't play it for people who aren't ready to listen to it. Don't play it for critical friends or family. Play it for people who will listen, appreciate, and applaud. It's also valuable to have a musically informed friend who will communicate honestly and kindly about your work without damaging your sensitive ego.

When I moved from Seattle to San Francisco, I fell in with a community of very creative jazz musicians. I was writing songs and occasionally performed them in little coffeehouse gigs, but most of my energy was spent learning about jazz. The musicians I met and sang with were vastly more advanced musically than I was, and my greatest education came from rehearsing and performing with them. I was always asking questions about the music, and the instrumentalists I worked with were generous in teaching me the fundamentals. During the 1980s I was also singing in a wedding band, and the band members were all jazz musicians who thought that playing casuals (private events) would be a fun way to make some money. I was the junior member regarding musical knowledge, but these guys had an admirable work ethic and even when they were masquerading as tuxedo-clad rock stars, they were adamant about doing things correctly. I had my "book" of charts for standards that were always part of the dinner jazz first set at a wedding reception, and I was duly informed if the changes weren't correct. I learned how to write a good chart and began to pursue some actual instruction in jazz theory.

My original songs kept coming but had become my closet passion that not many of the musicians I worked with even knew about. Eventually, the secret came out and a group of guys in the wedding band agreed to play the tunes with me in a coffeehouse setting. I was thrilled at their interest and we did a few gigs in nondescript venues which were surprisingly well received. My big moment came when I scored a gig at Yoshi's, the favorite jazz club in Oakland, in the early 1990s. I was terrified. I remember agonizing over my fear of presenting my songs to the sophisticated audience that attended the Jazz in Flight *series and fantasized about ways to get out of doing the gig. I even imagined throwing myself down the stairs and breaking a bone so I wouldn't have to do it. Crazy, I know, but the fear of revealing my secret songs to a critical and musically sophisticated audience was overwhelming. My strategy was to dive into my fear, to put my head in the lion's mouth. I would force myself to daydream a worst case scenario, like playing to an empty room, or having people laugh, or boo, or walk out on me. I trembled with shame at the thought and pushed my inner terrors so far that eventually it became comical. I came back to Earth and realized that it probably wasn't going to come to that. By the time I went onstage the night of the show, I was calm and ready to sing. The audience was very receptive, and some came up to me after the show and thanked me for the music. I went home and stayed awake all night. The gig at Yoshi's was a turning point for me. I walked on air for weeks and finally realized that my original music had a place in the world.*

A couple of years after the Yoshi's gig I made my first studio album, "The Postcard", and fell in love with the process of recording. It's exciting to sing for an audience, but I love the precision and focus of the studio. And unlike a home computer demo, you get to work with other people, especially a recording engineer, which is another level of quality that's hard to create on your own. I also love that you can make the music reflect the way you hear it in your head, like painting with sound, complete with the option of do-overs when it isn't quite right. Documenting your original songs in an optimal recording situation may be one of the most satisfying self-validations of the work you have strived to actualize. When you think of all the years of creativity that are surrounded by clouds of question marks about your worthiness as an artist, taking the step to go into a professional recording studio is a move to the next level of your artistic life. I highly recommend it as an important tool in building your career as a songwriter. Having a few professional albums available for listening is an important part of booking gigs. When you take yourself seriously enough to invest the time and money in the production of an album of your music, you are making a statement about your confidence and your belief in your own creative voice. When you are ready, your experience in the studio will likely be more fun than you can imagine, and you will come out of it a better musician than you were when you went in. Inspiration, notebooks of ideas, composition, meticulous translation of your songs to written notation, sharing your music with other musicians, refining your performance, performing often for audiences who listen, making high quality recordings and releasing them into the world, are all part of the wonderful journey of making your own music. If you don't believe in yourself, who will?

Tips

1. Somebody once said that the definition of insanity is doing the same thing over and over and expecting different results. If that's true, then good musicians are truly insane. We must practice if we want to master our musical expressions, whatever they are, and that means doing the same thing over and over. Being disciplined in your solo practice time is a very beneficial habit to develop. When you work with other musicians, you want to be an asset to the game by being able to play or sing as well as possible.

2. Rehearsal with other musicians, for performances or recordings is essential. Even great musicians who can read your impeccable charts will need to try on the music and find the essence of it with repetitions of the material. With your original tunes you want to create the best versions you can. This is another reason for being fluent in the language of music. Being able to direct traffic with precise terminology ensures that time is not wasted while traveling to the destination. Plan and run your rehearsals like a pro, and everyone will have more fun.

3. Respect the musicians you work with. Pay them fairly for their time and communicate your directions with patience and consideration. Being professional means being clear in what you ask for and courteous when something needs to be clarified.

4. Make sure your charts are accurate and legible. Whether they are handwritten or computer generated, don't be sloppy in the way the material is organized. The chart should reflect an accurate map and be easy to read, and your verbal instructions should be economical and correct. You know what you mean, but the rest of the band can't read your mind.

5. Playing music with other people is one of the most fun things you can do. If you do your part and show up prepared, you can relax and enjoy the process. Food also helps. Not kidding here. When rehearsing or recording, I always plan for breaks and provide refreshments. It makes everyone happier. When the band is happy, they play better, and that makes me happy.

6. Studio recordings and professional videos are expensive. The music business is in a rather bleak state regarding compensation for time spent creating product. However, I have never considered the dubious monetary returns for performing or recording a deal breaker when the making of the music is so divinely satisfying and worth every bit of the energy it requires.

9
CODA

This final section contains a few short subjects, some of which have been mentioned briefly in previous pages. I am choosing to revisit them with a little more detail here to underscore their importance in the whole picture of writing songs. This book is by no means exhaustive in its approach to songwriting, but everything mentioned here has crossed my path in my own musical adventures.

Songwriting Methods and Instruction

Recently I had a very interesting conversation with a prominent instructor of songwriting who has written a few books. He offers well attended workshops around the country and is considered an expert on the subject. Our exchange revealed some fundamental differences in our philosophical perspectives regarding creative work. His approach is to encourage students to think primarily about how their audiences will receive the songs they create. His view is that the success of a song is largely determined by how many people love it, how many buy it, how many cover it, how many attend performances to hear it, how many awards it receives, and how well it fits into the common practice templates of popular music. According to him, a song that is sophisticated and artistic but does not have mass crowd appeal is not a successful song no matter how beautiful, expressive, deep, or well-crafted it is. Writing for the sake of your own artistic expression is considered self-indulgent, while your purpose as a songwriter, first and foremost, is to reach, entertain, and uplift the listener. Apparently, many of his students have songs that are placed in television shows and movies and get played frequently on streaming platforms. I'm not one to argue with success, but I want to offer another point of view.

I have listed some of my favorite songwriters, and while some are not well known, several of them grew into broad audience appeal over the years. What attracted me to their music in the first place was their choice to take the road less traveled in their creative work. I have certainly loved many popular tunes but find that I am most captivated by music that moves beyond the limitations of commercial product. My immersion in jazz has expanded this preference. I love adventurous melody and harmony, surprising forms, and lyrics that are bold and imaginative. In other words, I am drawn to music that is intelligent, personal, original, and true. When my younger brother came to one of my concerts while he was in town visiting, he listened politely. As we were walking to the sushi restaurant after the show, he turned to me and said "I don't get your music". Sigh. I have been writing for my own taste for the past couple of decades. Studying and performing many styles of music has been a wonderful education, but my intention as a songwriter is to search my own heart and soul for what is meaningful and beautiful to me, and to craft my songs from this inspiration to the best of my ability. Of course, it's profoundly satisfying when people like my songs. Of course, I enjoy the applause and the compliments from other musicians and the listeners who come to my concerts. But I also love playing my songs all by myself and marveling at the miracle of music that has chosen to express itself through me. I never think in terms of "hit" songs or broad popularity. I just write songs because songwriting is one of my favorite things to do.

You will decide which direction you want to take in developing your original music. You may have long range goals going forward that include commercial success. You may seek to master the styles that are popular and appeal to huge audiences and compete for placements and awards. Or you may choose to live within an artistic framework that has different measurements for success. Music is available to everyone who wants to experience it, for any reason they choose to. I know what I prefer, but taste is personal. There is no right or wrong in seeking instruction from any point of view regarding your creative expression. I recommend that you see what's out there and take what you can from all kinds of methods and teachers to find out what informs your own unique musical voice.

The Hack

We live in the era of immediate gratification. Rewards are just a few clicks away. With the right app, we can replicate a facsimile of an experience without having to deeply study the components of that experience. The reliance on prefab loops instead of composed chord progressions gives the songwriter the feeling of having written something, even if their personal contribution to the process was only one or two aspects of it. But this negligence in composition often results in amorphous blobs of sound that sort of resemble music.

I sometimes have a hard time convincing my students that music is a study and practice that has tremendous depth, many levels and tendrils, and is extremely gratifying if you take the dive into its treasure laden waters. When you realize that notes on the staff have corresponding sounds that can take your breath away, aren't you curious? Don't you want to play with the big kids? I always found the study of music to be inherently captivating. And since I was a professional performing musician, I had to develop a strong work ethic in order to share the bandstand with the incredible musicians I was working with. I studied and practiced diligently and acquired the skills that got me in the door, into the bands, teaching in the conservatory, and performing on concert stages.

Studying and practicing all facets of music, becoming fluent in the language, and having some level of skill on your instrument takes time. The payoff is being in the game instead of watching it from the outside. Skip the hacks and do the work.

The Hook: Is It Necessary?

Some songwriting methods suggest starting the writing process by creating a hook and working backwards from there. But what exactly is a hook? It's the high point in a song, a few bars of music that are irresistibly exciting, the obvious and unmistakable feel-good part of the song, the distilled essence of the content of the writing, regardless of the subject matter or style. It usually occurs in the chorus, as a moment of release after an increase in the dynamic tension of the pre-chorus and makes everything else that happened previously in the song seem like it was always headed to this destination point. In fact, the sections of the song that precede the hook may be intentionally simplistic and energetically moderate in order to create contrast with the impact of the high-intensity chorus where the hook lives. Lyrically, it often contains the title of the song. A great hook is considered solid gold in pop music, and it's easy to understand why. It doesn't, and in fact shouldn't, require much thought to enjoy it. It's a visceral experience, carefully timed and constructed to produce an emotional and physical response, chills, euphoria, the urge to sing along, and it's usually a necessary component of any hit song. A few songs that come to mind that are dazzling with great hooks: "Tiny Dancer" by Elton John (with Bernie Taupin), "Ain't Nobody" by Chaka Kahn (written by Hawk Wolinski), "Rolling in the Deep" by Adele (with Paul Epworth), "Bad Guy" by Billy Eilish (with her brother Finneas), "Happy" by Pharrell Williams, and "Natural Woman" by Aretha Franklin (written by Carol King).

There are songwriting instructors who are well versed in the components and necessity of hook-making, but I'm not one of them. I'm not a proponent of formulaic concoctions of emotion designed to grab the listener, but I appreciate them when they are well done, and sometimes find that I have included them in my songs. The best ones have a spontaneous feel that is energetically alive and magnetic. And since emotion is the most important element in a song for me, I like it when a song starts somewhere, travels a distance, and gives answers to the "what's it all about?" question. But creating a mood that is less defined by the obvious signpost of a chorus with a hook can also qualify as great songwriting if the other components are intentional and well crafted. Your audience may have sophisticated ears and have no need for a mainline dopamine boost to understand and appreciate your music. There are many ways to generate an emotional response in music that don't rely on a single destination that dominates the song. As I'm writing, I observe my own response to the music throughout the tune. I want everything to feel good, to feel right, to feel balanced and dynamic.

You can create a world in a song that generates feeling on many levels throughout, even if there is not a single explosive sledge-hammer destination. A chord progression has countless possibilities for combining sounds that interact and create an atmosphere. Melodies that are crafted intentionally will contain levels of dynamic interest, unlike the path-of-least-resistance approach to melody often found in pop music. Lyrics also have tremendous power to reach the listener with imagery and meaning. Some of the songwriters I revere, like Joni Mitchell, Laura Nyro, many of the composers and lyricists of the Tin Pan Alley period, music that comes from Brazil and other world music cultures, musical theater, and contemporary jazz composition do not always rely on a hook to evoke a response in the listener. Even without the hook as a grand prize, we can still write with dynamic intention, creating highs and lows, tension and release, contrasting levels of intensity, and conscious choice in crafting the details. Again, I go back to my initial approach to songwriting that starts with an understanding of what you are writing about, a broad musical vocabulary and skill set, and the willingness to handle each detail with care so that the emotional content of the song comes to life.

Collaboration

I've always been a solo songwriter, probably because of my tendency toward control freakism. But there are countless songwriting teams who have found the necessary rapport to create good, cohesive music together. Songwriting teams created much of the music that came out of the Tin Pan Alley years, and Broadway musicals are often the work of multiple writers. Pop music writers also write in teams, and sometimes a single song lists several names in the writing credits. In jazz you will often see songs that were written instrumentally, with lyrics that were added later so singers could perform them. I marvel at this ability to cooperate and agree on final choices in lyrics and music. If you are inclined to play well with others, collaborating might be very enjoyable. If you have songwriting partners who complement your talents, whose taste you trust, who can be diplomatically critical, and contribute equally to the process, this could be a very productive, inspiring and fun way to create songs. Just remember to give credit to everyone who contributes anything to the creation of the song.

Rewriting and Discarding

There is no harm in working a song into the ground and just not being able to save it from the bin. You may be certain that you're starting with a good idea, and yet not be able follow through to a satisfactory completion. Nevertheless, the time you spend working on any music is time well spent, and never wasted. If a song functions as an exercise in tripped out harmony, or a difficult time signature, then you are increasing your skill set just working on it. I often rewrite my songs, sometimes completing them very differently from where I started. Now and then I discard them altogether. This often comes after compositional banging of my head against the wall, trying to eke out something musically and just running out of ideas. Finally, if I get to the point where I realize that the song is just not that fun to sing, I let it go. Occasionally I plunder a chart I previously tossed out and grab a phrase or a section and place it in another song. It's probably wise to hang onto music that may never be performed, just in case it may hold an idea or two that can be placed in a new project. Hey, it's my stuff and I can use it wherever I want. I recently wrote a ballad that blissed me out while I was in the process, but I sang it a few times with a couple of different accompanists, and it fell flat. Months went by and I found it again in my stack of charts. When I played it as a slightly faster jazz waltz, and changed the key, it came together surprisingly well.

Grow Your Skills

You can do a lot with what you know, and you can do more if you know more. You can create a beautiful painting with a few tubes of paint but what a blast it is to have a full array of colors to smoosh around on your palette. Some of us have had the gift of early exposure to piano lessons, choir, even playing in a high school garage band. This does create a foundation for hearing things in a musical way, but the knowledge is out there for people who don't quite speak the language at a conversational level. I did not go to music school, nor do I have a degree in music, but I have been playing and singing since I was a child. Much of my adult life was spent in the company of musicians who were vastly more advanced than me and I availed myself of their knowledge. I took lots of private lessons from master instructors and asked them questions that were pertinent to what I was trying to do. When I studied classical singing in my 20s I developed the habit of practicing 3 hours a day, 6 days a week. This discipline stuck with me and helped me to improve my skills. I needed help with my vocal technique, theory, composition, improvisation, arranging, recording, and performance. I was very motivated to learn this stuff because the music was beating on the doors of my soul trying to get out. You are never too old to learn in the service of your heart's expression. Check out the private instructors and classes available to adult students. The knowledge is waiting for you if you are motivated to reach for it.

Criticism

OUCH!! Yes, it's hard to hear negative comments about your work, but you have some choices here. Friends and family may represent the general public and their opinions might give you an idea of how well your songs will go over when they are released into the world, but take their comments with a grain of salt. Some listeners might not appreciate music that is subtle or unfamiliar sounding and instead prefer simplicity and overt adherence to trends. Toss out a blues or something with a heavy hook and a good dance groove and it will be well received because it's recognizable.

When you start to get adventurous with your tunes you may want to save them for more discriminating ears when you want feedback. Take your songs to those who have the experience and knowledge to recognize the quality of your music, and who can help problem solve if something isn't working. Workshops with other songwriters can be of great value, especially if the instructor has the skills to nudge you in the right direction when you get stuck. A good teacher will know how to help you without making you feel stupid, and hearing the comments from others in the workshop can be especially valuable.

If you are at the performance level that draws reviews, brace yourself for critique that isn't always affirmative. Remember, people whose job it is to write reviews are not omniscient about the value of music, and sometimes seem to be more in love with their own writing than opening their ears to something new. If you get a bad review you may learn something about the strengths and weaknesses of your work, but don't take it to heart. I don't admonish self-criticism in the writing process unless it's compulsive and unrelenting. Being critical of your artistic work means you care about it and have high standards. If something isn't working in your songs, be honest and address the weak points with different choices. I write my music in such a way that I love all of it. I am meticulous about every choice I make and don't stop working on it until I'm satisfied. When I'm too lazy to do this, it nags at me until I take care of it. I know that not everyone will love every song I write, but when I know I've done my best and the work is good in my own opinion, I'm not so vulnerable to the opinions of others.

Copyright

Your original songs belong to you, and you want to own them legally. Copyrighting your material is a fairly simple process and protects you from anyone stealing your work. You will need to have accurate documentation of your songs in written and/or recorded form, plus all the information about who did what in relation to lyrics, music, arranging, recording, etc. Then you go the U.S. government's copyright website, *copyright.gov*, and create an account. The walk through is pretty straightforward with step-by-step instructions. You will be asked to pay the fees before you upload your work. The "poor man's copyright", mailing yourself a copy of your song and leaving the envelope sealed is not absolute legal protection. There are online legal services if you feel the need to get some help in doing this correctly. After copyrighting your work, it might be a good idea to join a performance rights organization like BMI or ASCAP. In the same way that you are required to pay licensing fees when you record someone else's song, you should be paid if someone records your song. If you are releasing an album, copyrighting your songs is essential.

The Younger Generation

As it has always been, the popular music in American culture is defined by young people. My musical awakening came with the Beatles' arrival in my sonic consciousness when I was a teenager. I hardly recognize the names of many of the currently popular artists and I thank my students for introducing me to the popular songs and songwriters that continue to emerge.

Some of the newer methods of song creation didn't exist when I started writing songs. Sampling, loops, beats, etc., are a kind of song construction that made me wonder, where is the line between sampling and plagiarism? Is looping merely a machine generated gimmick that is going to grow tiresome when the novelty wears off? But upon hearing the creative things that people are doing with these approaches it's clear that, as in all art, the good stuff is in the mind of the artist. Creating with care and intention may require a different skill set than it once did, but those who create in these idioms have learned to use technology to explore and experiment with music for the early 21st Century. The history of music has always been a history of changing trends from one generation to the next. Subject matter and content are both the same and different from music of the past. While inspiration is often reflective of the world we live in (dystopian, confused, and yet hopeful), romantic relationship angst seems universal to every generation and central to lyrical themes.

In this age of the "hack", shortcuts to an artistic destination, there seems to be less interest in the acquisition of traditional musical skills than I would prefer. But young jazz musicians are as dedicated as ever to the acquisition of knowledge, chops, and experience, with the intention of becoming well-rounded and broadly informed musicians. In the realm of pop and alternative styles, I've heard some very expressive young singer/songwriters who are creating deep and arresting lyrics but give very little attention to creative chord progressions or melody. It's refreshing to hear the exceptions, music that is fresh and interesting, with care and attention given to melodic and harmonic content along with meaningful lyrics.

In terms of innovativeness, the word of the day in newer music is: *Hybrid*. I love how traditional styles have morphed over the years making old things sound new. A groove here, a progression there, an approach to form, things are borrowed from established styles and combined in ways that are intriguing and exciting. In jazz, you are hearing a lot of older pop music given a jazz treatment, with reharmonization and more sophisticated grooves. The wonderful musical collaboration project that goes by the name of "Playing for Change" has incorporated classic pop and R&B tunes with world rhythms, and featured musicians from all over the world in recorded videos. In a single song you might hear blues singer, Taj Mahal, with classical cellist, Yo-yo Ma. When Billy Childs created his tribute album to Laura Nyro, the opening song was sung by classical singer, Renee Fleming, and several other new and established vocal artists contributed renditions of Laura's stunning songs. A well-established music collective in Oakland, CA , led by Adam Theis, is called The Jazz Mafia, and they continue to expand the definitions of style, bringing in artists from different genres to create music that is original and exhilarating. Groups like Snarky Puppy, or the Metropole Orchestra present featured artists performing their original songs in elaborate arrangements with multiple musicians. I'm a huge fan of Jacob Collier, a young British prodigy, multi-instrumentalist and composer who has boundless energy and imagination. Hiatus Kaiyote is an Australian jazz funk band with a very original sound, led by singer/composer Nai Palm. Another favorite of mine is the very creative singer/songwriter and instrumentalist, Becca Stevens, who writes jazz/pop tunes that are beautifully arranged and emotionally dimensional. Esperanza Spalding is a young bassist/singer/composer. She is a stunning musician, at home improvising on jazz standards and performing original music that is sophisticated and moving. It's exciting to hear young musicians who are in command of all aspects of the music they are writing and performing.

There will always be stuff we can't stand and stuff we love, and that's a reality that is timeless. Many facets of popular music are deep, original, expressive, and enjoyable to listen to. And there is also an overwhelming amount of mindless noise that was created as product to be sold to undiscriminating audiences. This has always been the case in popular music. What is common to the newer music that stands out and rises above the noise, in any genre, is the same thing I love about all good music. It makes me feel something. Although young people today live in a world that is very different from the one I grew up in, human emotion, and the desire to express it through art, is fundamental to human life.

Talent

This is a controversial subject, but I don't think enough is said about it in this modern world where everyone is a star in somebody's sky. Yes, your mom is proud of everything you do, well almost everything, but people are born with different interests and aptitudes. Musical aptitude is not uncommon. Everyone in my family was born with a decent singing voice, and fundamental musicality – good intonation and strong rhythmic comprehension. I was the only one in a family of six who developed a career in music, but they all love to sing, and both of my brothers play the guitar well enough to accompany themselves. When I started piano lessons in grade school, learning the basics was a breeze, and my later studies of music theory made complete sense to me without much effort. If this sounds like a brag, it's not. There are so many things in life that baffle me, and I am overflowing with appreciation for people who possess skills and aptitudes that I lack. Musical aptitude was something that I was born with, through no fault of my own, but I'm a lousy cook and am seriously befuddled by computer technology, and so much more.

Talent is another level of aptitude. Most of the artists who achieve greatness in their chosen medium have a special quality that stands out, a kind of inspired magnetism, something that lights up like a beacon and makes people want to stand in their radiance. They still work hard, but it's like the path before them is littered with those old fashioned cut-outs of feet that were once used for dance instructions, pointing the way and guiding them toward the actualization of their gifts. They don't have to beg for attention because their audiences want to be there drinking up the elixir of their expression. Among the general population, even among those with high aptitude, great artists are rare. We know them when we hear them and are humbled by their wondrous ability to transform the very air that surrounds them.

Aptitude and talent exist on a spectrum. I have had many music students who lacked aptitude and even when their desire was great, music did not give them much return for their investment. I never discourage anyone from enjoying music at whatever level they can, but sometimes I hope that students will find another avenue of expression that will come more easily. I have also worked with students who were shockingly gifted but who eventually gave up the pursuit of excellence and achievement in music because they wanted other things from life – like being able to pay the bills. Where do you fit in this mix? It's hard to say what can be achieved with dedication and high aptitude. When I compared myself in my 20s to Joni Mitchell in her 20s, the outlook was bleak. Nevertheless, without actually choosing music, it became the framework of my life. When I put one foot in front of the other, the road always seemed to lead to music – not stardom, but the practice of music. I tried many facets of the music life and it seemed that my personal niche was writing songs. I worked at writing the best songs I could imagine and that has given me a satisfying life, a purpose that has been actualized.

I come back now to where I started at the beginning of this book. Finding the love in whatever we do with our time is the point of doing it. Working with personal authenticity, discipline, and integrity, to harness our inspiration and craft, to the best of our ability, not stopping until we know we've done our very best, is a good enough reason to keep on doing it. This may or may not result in recognition by others. I know many musicians whom I considered highly talented and accomplished. They perform often, are in high demand, their audiences sometimes flock to their gigs, and sometimes they play before an audience of 7 people. If they are not necessarily known on the world stage, they are known by other musicians who appreciate them. Sometimes there is great joy in participating within a community of artists who recognize each other's gifts and provide a feeling of belonging, a rightness of purpose, and space to share these sounds that must be heard.

Finally

Musicians are a tribe, and we, you and me, are part of it. Music chose us and we are its emissaries in the world. Even if no one ever hears the music we create, the act of creating it can make us deeper and more dimensional human beings than we might otherwise be. Music is an ephemeral thing. It's played into the air and disappears, but we can learn to capture it and contain it in our writing and recording of it, making it an offering we can pass on to others. If your only musical skill is the ability to sing a song while walking alone on a beach or a path through the woods, sing out! You are making music. And when you pursue the study and practice of it, your skills and enjoyment will grow. It will keep you company when you are lonely, and it will take the walk with you into the later years of your life. When you make music with other people, you share an intimate and expansive exchange of energy that warms you long after it's over. I encourage you to cherish your musical gift and to know that it is one of the puzzle pieces that finds its place in the realm of art, of community, of heritage, of grief and celebration, among the voices of humanity. Nature sings the songs of birds, wolves, whales, insects, frogs, rain and thunder, and the hiss of the wind in the leaves. We're part of this. So much of what we do here in our time upon the Earth leaves behind a mess. Music comes from the ether, travels through our voices and instruments, and puts vibration into the air that changes the energetic quality of our experience for the better. It's a gift and a responsibility. Give it your time, give it your love, and it will love you back. If your song makes one person smile or shed a tear of deep feeling, it's worth the time and effort it took to bring it into the world.

APPENDIX

The next few pages contain lists of songwriters, songwriting teams, and lyricists I would like to recommend to the readers of this book. Each exemplifies work that is exceptional in the field of original music. This is not an encyclopedia or a textbook, so I have limited my choices to those who have stood out for me personally. Even under that label, many I admire are not listed here. I hope you will listen to songs on my lists that are not familiar to you. I have taken care to represent many styles and several decades from the 20th and 21st Centuries.

I have also compiled a short list of resources that you may find helpful in your study and pursuit of songwriting.

Songwriters (Composer/Lyricists)

This alphabetized list includes songwriters who have made an impact on my life and my writing. This is by no means an exhaustive list of great songwriters. I chose those whose work I'm familiar with and who represent, for me, the art and craft of songwriting. Many genres comprise this list, and each songwriter mentioned has written multiple songs that are exceptional. If you don't recognize some of these names, I highly recommend checking them out. Most of them perform their own songs, and many of the songs have been covered by other artists. They will inspire you, make you cry, make you fall in love, dance, and make you wish you had written that song (as I so often do).

Mose Allison:
Everybody's Cryin' Mercy
Lost Mind
Your Mind is on Vacation
Your Molecular Structure

Fiona Apple:
Paper Bag
Not About Love
Fast as You Can
Hot Knife

Irving Berlin:
Say it Isn't So
Let's Face the Music and Dance
What'll I Do?
Puttin' On the Ritz

Leonard Cohen:
Hallelujah
Anthem
Suzanne
Dance Me to the End of Love

Jacob Collier:
The Sun Is In Your Eyes
Time to Rest Your Weary Head
In the Real Early Morning
Make Me Cry

Donovan:
Catch the Wind
Epistle to Dippy
Young Girl Blues
Widow With a Shawl

Bob Dorough:
Devil May Care
Small Day Tomorrow
Love Came on Stealthy Fingers
But for Now

Bob Dylan:
Like a Rolling Stone
Make You Feel My Love
The Times They Are A-Changin'
You're Gonna Make Me Lonesome When You Go

APPENDIX

Billy Eilish:
Bad Guy
No Time to Die
When the Party's Over
Ocean Eyes

Donald Fagen:
Aja
The Goodbye Look
Deacon Blues
I.G.Y.

Dave Frishberg:
I'm Hip
My Attorney Bernie
Blizzard of Lies
You Are There (With Johnny Mandel)

Antonio Carlos Jobim:
Children's Games
The Waters of March
Correnteza
Triste

Rickie Lee Jones:
We Belong Together
Youngblood
Living It Up
Skeletons

Abbey Lincoln:
Throw It Away
Living Room (with Max Roach)
The Music is the Magic
Bird Alone

John Mayer:
Stop This Train
3x5
City Love
Free Fallin'

Paul McCartney:
Here, There, and Everywhere
Eleanor Rigby
Michelle
For No One

Michael McDonald:
What a Fool Believes
Minute by Minute
I Can Let Go Now
Takin' It to the Streets

Joni Mitchell:
Hejira
River
A Case of You
Blue

Van Morrison:
Brown Eyed Girl
Moondance
Into the Mystic
Crazy Love

Milton Nacimiento:
Ponta De Areia
Tarde
Cancao do Sal
Bandieras

Randy Newman:
I Think It's Gonna Rain Today
Sail Away
Marie
You've Got a Friend In Me

Laura Nyro:
Eli's Comin'
Captain for Dark Mornings
Upstairs by a Chinese Lamp
And When I Die

Cole Porter:
Every Time We Say Goodbye
So in Love
All of You
I Concentrate On You

Paul Simon:
America
The Boxer
Bridge Over Troubled Water
50 Ways to Leave Your Lover

Stephen Sondheim:
Not While I'm Around
I Remember
Loving You
Send In the Clowns

Esperanza Spalding:
I Know You Know
Apple Blossom
Radio Song
Unconditional Love

Becca Stevens:
Weightless
Regina
Traveler's Blessing
For You the Night is Still

Sting:
Fields of Gold
Fragile
Brand New Day
Sister Moon

James Taylor:
Copperline
Sweet Baby James
Don't Let Me Be Lonely Tonight
You Can Close Your Eyes

Tom Waits:
Take it With Me
Lookin for the Heart of Saturday Night
San Diego Serenade
Hold on

Jimmy Webb:
Wichita Lineman
By the Time I Get to Phoenix
The Moon is a Harsh Mistress
Up Up and Away

Wendy Waldman:
Mad Mad Me
Wild Bird
Strange Company
Mr. Boatman

APPENDIX

Stevie Wonder:
You and I
As
Living for the City
Overjoyed

Neil Young:
After the Goldrush
Don't Let It Bring You Down
The Needle and the Damage Done
Cowgirl in the Sand

Songwriting Teams

Countless exceptional songs have been written by composer/lyricist collaborators. While we tend to focus on one or the other, sometimes giving full credit for the creation of a song by the most recognizable name in the team, I'm a firm believer in giving credit where it's due. Various genres and time periods are represented here, and again, this is a condensed list.

Burt Bacharach/Hal David:
Alfie
I Say a Little Prayer
Anyone Who Had a Heart
What the World Needs Now is Love

George and Ira Gershwin:
Love Walked In
Love is Here to Stay
Embraceable You
Liza

Elton John/Bernie Taupin:
Your Song
Tiny Dancer
Goodbye Yellow Brick Road
Rocket Man

Jerome Kern:
The Way You Look Tonight/Dorothy Fields
All the Things You Are/Oscar Hammerstein
The Song is You/Oscar Hammerstein
Can't Help Lovin' That Man/Oscar Hammerstein

Michel Legrand/Marilyn and Alan Bergman:
The Summer Knows
The Windmills of Your Mind
You Must Believe in Spring
What Are You Doing the Rest of Your Life?

Ivan Lins/Vitor Martins (Portuguese):
Comecar de Novo (The Island – Marilyn/Alan Bergman)
Daquilo Que Eu Sei (Believe What I Say – Patti Austin)
Velas Icadas (Sails – Gene Lees)
Lembranca (Love Dance – Paul Williams)

John Lennon/Paul McCartney:
A Day in the Life
Norwegian Wood
All My Loving
Paperback Writer

Henry Mancini:
Moon River/Johnny Mercer
Charade/Johnny Mercer
Two for the Road/Leslie Bricusse
Dreamsville/Ray Evans, Jay Livingston

APPENDIX

Johnny Mandel:
Close Enough for Love/Paul Williams
Emily/Johnny Mercer
The Shadow of Your Smile/Paul Francis Webster
A Time for Love/Paul Francis Webster

Anthony Newley/Leslie Bricusse:
Once in a Lifetime
Feeling Good
Pure Imagination
Who Can I Turn To?

Lyricists

Language is often the bridge between the listener and the composer, and a creative and well-crafted lyric can make a great piece of music even more accessible to an audience. In fact, sometimes the lyrics are more memorable than the music. Lyricists know that songs are usually inspired by experiences and feelings, and in a good song, words *are* music. Words can be rapture. These lyricists are a few of my favorites, and it's notable that several are also singers who perform and record with their collaborators.

Laurie Antonioli:
Varuna (Richie Beirach)
Layla (Nguyen Le)
Soulmates (Fritz Pauer)
Flamenco Sketches (Miles Davis)

Marilyn and Alan Bergman:
You Must Believe in Spring (Michel Legrand)
The Island (Ivan Lins)
In the Heat of the Night (Quincy Jones)
The Way We Were (Marvin Hamlisch)

Leslie Bricusse:
Feeling Good (Anthony Newley)
Pure Imagination (Anthony Newley)
And We Were Lovers (Jerry Goldsmith)
Two For the Road (Henry Mancini)

Kurt Elling:
Where I Belong (Laurence Hobgood)
Minuano (Pat Metheny/Lyle Mays)
Resolution (John Coltrane)
Time to Say Goodbye (Joe Zawinul)

Lorraine Feather:
A Hopeful Note (Dave Grusin)
Life Story (Shelly Berg)
Grand Invention (Russell Ferrante)
I Always Had a Thing for You (Arkin, Berg, Ferrante, Fleck, Hyman)

Dorothy Fields:
The Way You Look Tonight (Jerome Kern)
The Sunnyside of the Street (Jimmy McHugh)
Where Am I Going? (Cy Coleman)
Pick Yourself Up (Jerome Kern)

John Hendricks:
Joy Spring (Clifford Brown)
Reflections (Thelonious Monk)
Four (Miles Davis)
In Walked Bud (Thelonious Monk)

Gene Lees:
Turn Out the Stars (Bill Evans)
Desifinado (Antonio Carlos Jobim)
Bridges (Milton Nacimiento)
Waltz for Debby (Bill Evans

APPENDIX

Johnny Mercer:
Blues in the Night (Harold Arlen)
Moon River (Henry Mancini)
Skylark (Hoagy Carmichael)
I Thought About You (Jimmy Van Heusen)

Norma Winstone:
The Peacocks / A Timeless Place (Jimmy Rowles)
Ladies in Mercedes (Steve Swallow)
A Wish (Fred Hirsch)
Westerly (Ralph Towner)

RESOURCES

The following lists may help you further your growth as a songwriter. Fill your mind and your senses with diversity in music, in poetry, in your observations and explorations of life and the people you see and know. Analyze the songs you love and define what makes them special to you. Do the work that opens up your fluency in music theory, and in playing your instruments. Learn music notation and how to record yourself. Take lessons, classes, and workshops. Attend salons and open mics where you can perform your material. Keep songwriting journals, and always have paper and a pen somewhere on your person in case inspiration strikes.

Books

There are zillions of books about music, and my list here are my own personal well-thumbed favorites. Sher Music and Hal Leonard are great resources for *Fakebooks*. You can't have too many, especially those that are thoughtfully compiled with great chord changes. This is the list of books I personally own and have used frequently:

DICTIONARY – Webster Merriam
THESAURUS – Webster Merriam
RHYMING DICTIONARY – Gene Lees
HARPER'S DICTIONARY OF MUSIC – Christine Ammer
A HISTORY OF WESTERN MUSIC – Grout and Palisca
THE JAZZ THEORY BOOK – Mark Levine
THE STANDARDS REAL BOOK – Sher Music
VOCAL TECHNIQUE/PERFORMANCE – Ann Peckham
MODUS VETUS – Lars Edlund (sightsinging)
WRITING MUSIC FOR HIT SONGS – Jai Josefs*
SONGWRITING WITHOUT BOUNDARIES – Pat Pattison*

Tools

DIGITAL PIANO
NOTATION SOFTWARE (FINALE)
RECORDING SOFTWARE (LOGIC PRO)
MANUSCRIPT PAPER, PENCIL, ERASER

Study

There are countless music schools, conservatories, community colleges and universities that have expansive music programs with highly skilled and inspiring teachers. You may choose to attend classes in person or online.

Private Instruction

I have loved most of the music classes I have taken but have received tremendous benefit from individual private instructors. A good teacher with whom you have a rapport can help you in a way that specifically addresses where you are with your music. I seemed to meet the right music teachers at the right time. It's a valuable relationship, for both student and teacher, and good teachers abound.

*Both of these books and authors contain substantial information about music theory (Jai Josefs) and lyric writing (Pat Pattison). I do not follow either author, but some of my students have recommended their work. It's always a good idea to explore many available resources.

THANK YOU

To my teachers, music making friends, master musicians who lift us, all makers and anyone who makes life better, true lifelong friends and the ones who came and went, the people who helped me do this, the people who are patient and fun, the ones who listened, all the singers, the muse, the moon, a long life woven through with shiny threads of music, the songs that came flying by right when I had my net handy.

ABOUT THE AUTHOR

During her career as a singer and singing teacher, Stephanie Bruce has performed in a range of styles, including folk, classical, pop, and jazz, all of which have informed her numerous original compositions. Her study of music began with piano lessons in grade school and continued with college classes, and private lessons in voice, piano, theory, music history, and composition. Her musical education was also greatly influenced by the stellar professional musicians who taught and encouraged her while sharing the stage. She has taught vocal technique, musicianship, repertoire development, performance, choral singing, and songwriting, privately and in classes, including over 10 years at the California Jazz Conservatory in Berkeley, CA. Stephanie has released three original albums, THE POSTCARD, APRIL IN DOGTOWN, and WHISPERS FROM THE WORLD NEXT DOOR. Without necessarily intending it to be so, music became the path, the framework, the companion, the light, the work, the comfort, the compass, the feast, and the flight. And it's not over yet.

CPSIA information can be obtained
at www.ICGtesting.com
Printed in the USA
JSHW011331200123
36283JS00003B/94